A LAYMAN'S VIEW OF HISTORY

By HENRY OSBORN TAYLOR

ANCIENT IDEALS. (*Two Volumes*)

CLASSICAL HERITAGE OF THE MIDDLE AGES

THE MEDIAEVAL MIND. (*Two Volumes*)

PROPHETS, POETS, AND PHILOSOPHERS OF THE ANCIENT WORLD

THOUGHT AND EXPRESSION IN THE SIXTEENTH CENTURY. (*Two Volumes*)

FREEDOM OF THE MIND IN HISTORY

HUMAN VALUES AND VERITIES

FACT: THE ROMANCE OF MIND

A LAYMAN'S VIEW OF HISTORY

A LAYMAN'S VIEW OF HISTORY

By

HENRY OSBORN TAYLOR

NEW YORK
THE MACMILLAN COMPANY
1935

COPYRIGHT, 1935,
BY HENRY OSBORN TAYLOR.

All rights reserved — no part of this book may be reproduced in any form without permission in writing from the publisher, except by a reviewer who wishes to quote brief passages in connection with a review written for inclusion in magazine or newspaper.

Set up and printed. Published March, 1935.

· PRINTED IN THE UNITED STATES OF AMERICA ·

PREFACE

The first piece, *A Layman's View of History*, was a presidential address delivered at Washington before The American Historical Association in December, 1927, and then printed in *The American Historical Review* and later in *Science*. It makes a proper title for this little collection of essays, several of which reflect a view of history that I have long thought upon. The next piece, *Old Age*, was written slowly in the last year or more, and has not been printed. *Mont-Saint-Michel and Chartres by Henry Adams* appeared in *The American Historical Review* in 1913, and *The Education of Henry Adams* in *The Atlantic Monthly* for October, 1918, the year of his death. *The Phi Beta Kappa Ideal* was read at the installation of a chapter of the Society at The Rice Institute of Houston in March, 1929, and was published in a Rice Institute Pamphlet.

The pieces written during the World War sprang from the thoughts and feelings of the

PREFACE

time. *The Pathos of America*, printed in *The Atlantic Monthly* for February, 1916, was an emotional utterance that drew sparks from many very different people, brought me letters even from lunatics, and was reprinted in large type on the front page of *The Saloniki News* issued by the British authorities in that unhappy place. *Sub Specie Æternitatis* followed in August, 1916, in the same magazine, and *The Wisdom of the Ages* was published in *The Yale Review* for October, 1917, just after the United States entered the war. It closes with glowing paragraphs which serve only to show the futility of hopes engendered by that time of storm and stress.

Henry Osborn Taylor

CONTENTS

	PAGE
A LAYMAN'S VIEW OF HISTORY	1
OLD AGE	24
THE EDUCATION OF HENRY ADAMS	49
MONT-SAINT-MICHEL AND CHARTRES	74
THE PHI BETA KAPPA IDEAL	81

PIECES WRITTEN DURING THE WAR

THE PATHOS OF AMERICA	103
SUB SPECIE ÆTERNITATIS	107
THE WISDOM OF THE AGES	116

A LAYMAN'S VIEW OF HISTORY

A LAYMAN'S VIEW OF HISTORY [1]

Some time ago I received a pleasant letter from an honored officer of our Association. Among other things he said that his friends and colleagues would be glad to have one more book from me telling how it was that I came to write history. He added friendly words as to the interest of professional teachers of history in the thoughts of laymen like myself. So I am moved to give you a layman's view of history.

The muster-roll of laymen who have written histories is not a mean one. The old world offers us Herodotus, Thucydides, Xenophon, Polybius, Tacitus, no one of whom held a chair at any university. In modern times, in England, we pass from Gibbon down to Grote, and, in our own country, from Parkman to Rhodes. For myself, hovering, as I faintly hope, somewhere on the fringe of this rather Olympian company, I will endeavor to answer

[1] Presidential address delivered before the American Historical Association at Washington, December 28, 1927.

in a few words the query in the very friendly letter.

When I was a young man I became bent on devoting my mind and energies to the best things I could find. Not having original and creative gifts, I set myself to the study of what other men had deemed best, and had striven to attain in thought and work and conduct. I had ardently studied law, had practised a very little, and had written a book on *Private Corporations*. But the law seemed too narrow — very far from covering the whole human field; and I turned to look beyond it. Being inclined toward the humanities rather than the sciences, I soon saw that I at least should find the most humanly interesting elements in the aim and the endeavor — the forming an ideal, and the struggle through the man's years, or perhaps through the longer life of a people, to accomplish it. The accomplishment itself, if indeed it is severable from the endeavor, might be beyond the strength either of individual or of race. Achievement lies on the knees of the gods. The true human story is a story of endeavor — the endeavor for the end conceived.

A LAYMAN'S VIEW OF HISTORY

So I began with the ancient world, which is the pit whence we have been digged. And I devoted the ten years that were my supreme education to writing *Ancient Ideals*. That brought my notion of the story down to the time of Christianity. I gave all my time to the book, working eight hours a day, and travelling to see some of the things and countries I was studying. I had very little money, but I used it, and at last sweated blood to pay for the publication of my work.

Then, with the advantage of this discipline of knowledge, I devoted four years to *The Classical Heritage of the Middle Ages*. During two of them, I held a lectureship at Columbia, but gave it up as interfering with my real work. Profiting by this further time of study and training, I next put ten enthusiastic years on *The Mediaeval Mind*, and, after that, six or seven years on *Thought and Expression in the Sixteenth Century*. There have been two or three smaller books, *Freedom of the Mind in History*, taking three years; and one that is now in the press bringing me to the present time.

Curiously enough I find that through all these books, if I have not been implicitly saying the same thing, I have, without intending it, been speaking with the voice of my first conviction as to the central human interest of the endeavor and the aim. Forty years, and all my mind and energy, have been put upon these books, which I mention to show the time they have taken. Such as they are, I could not have written them had my time been taken by teaching or academic administration. So much for this layman, now for his view of history.

Our ideas to-day of things about us are neither particular nor static. Rather we conceive a ceaseless movement to pervade the world; and we imagine that a like unbroken movement has brought all things to the present state of heterogeneous correlation as parts of a prodigiously variegated whole. Apparently it is one and the same universal movement that extends throughout our present world and reaches back through time. Within its sweep, past and present become a continuum, and our contemporary happenings are drawn into some real or conceptual unity. We recognize one vibrant current constituting

A LAYMAN'S VIEW OF HISTORY

an energizing and effective process. Each event is harnessed to the other, and the present emerges from the past. All seems an organic and possibly intelligent becoming. Perhaps this becoming is manifested most concretely in plants and animals. They *are* their past: phylogenetically as the present form of a somehow evolving species, and ontogenetically, since each living individual carries its line of ancestry to be handed on. These notions are not wholly new, yet they work in us to-day with new meaning.

If we turn from this universal process to our experience or knowledge of its phenomena, we find a like absence of barriers and separation. Fences are down between the fields of knowledge, which have become one vast *un*enclosure. Save for convenience of designation and prosecution, the sciences are no longer distinct and separate, but phases of each other, while philosophy would enfold them all in its consideration. Not unallied with them are philology, archaeology, all scholarship if you will. Indeed knowledge would conceivably become one, were there a mind genial enough to grasp it in its entirety.

A LAYMAN'S VIEW OF HISTORY

Every element of our knowledge of the present world of man and nature is necessarily connected with our knowledge of that past through which man and the world he lives in have come to be what they are. We need make no distinction between our knowledge of living animals and contemporary human institutions, and our knowledge of their antecedent stages. Every political or legal institution has come into existence gradually, or has arisen by notable mutation. The laws regulating corporations are of divers origin, yet there is continuity between the present body of corporation law and its multifarious past; and there need be no division in our knowledge of the past and present of this legal Briareus.

The continuity, or even oneness, between past and present is evident in the forms or provinces of knowledge. The science of physiology, for example, is a gradual and beautiful growth; its present state implies and includes its past, just as the animal organs, whose functions it treats of, contain their past genetically. Physics, so called, is also an emergence from its past, but more apparently by the way of mutation. Its fundamental conceptions appear to have suffered reversal. Yet if the old solidities of matter have been replaced by nimble units of electric energy, still the group of principles applying to the action of tangible bodies are as valid as they have ever been, and carry over the bulk of the science in its continuity. A more concrete illustration of mutation accompanying continuity is the manner in which relativity has, for a time at least, been grafted upon Newtonian gravitation.

And philosophy, that elastic method of ultimate consideration, of thinking any and all problems of the mind out to their final conclusions or despairs — this method or tissue of ultimate thinking assuredly becomes its whole self only in the oneness of its present with its past.

Yet changes come, and each age has its intellectual tendencies. Scientific or philosophic conceptions of the world are, of course, part of the thinking, even the temper, of a period. In modern physics the concepts of relativity and the substitution of electricity and motion for stolid matter are expressions of the spirit, the dynamic restlessness, of our times. So is our science of psychology, not to mention psychoanalysis specifically. A future age, with another temperament and mentality, may not be satisfied with them.

Knowledge is experience. But not all experience is knowledge, since experience may come in the guise of feeling or intuition. Such experience is direct, and is not apprehended through cognition and statement. Indeed much of our experience is rather untranslatable into knowledge or rational statement. Experience of the past, however, commonly takes the form of knowledge, or of doubt or conscious ignorance — the two latter being a mode of cognition or failure to know. Yet contemplation of a past event may stir our feeling and, as it were, arouse an intuitive sense of its import. To that extent our experience of the past might not take the form of knowledge.

In philosophy, realists and idealists still dispute as to the relation of all forms of experience to the assumed external world — the world past and present, I would add. Whatever be this relation, the point I wish to make is that our knowledge of the past and our knowledge

A LAYMAN'S VIEW OF HISTORY

of the present bear a like relation to the data or objects of their respective worlds. Knowledge of the past is the same sort of absorption or mirror of events as knowledge of the present. And if in any way knowledge of the present world should be held to reach practical identity with the assumed objective data, so one might hold as to knowledge of the past.

Again, as each man's knowledge, or other experience, of the present differs from that of his fellows, so will his knowledge of the past. This is strikingly true of historians living in different ages. Each age, with its own interests and view of life, will find in the past a different range of facts and interests. To different succeeding ages the past will appear, and even *be*, different.

As touching the intellectual identity in us of past and present, we should distinguish between evident forms of knowledge, like the sciences, and the material, for example, of past politics and war. The scholar may identify his knowledge of philosophy with philosophy's past as well as present, but will pause before identifying the Battle of Waterloo with his knowledge of it. In this respect, I should

A LAYMAN'S VIEW OF HISTORY

group religion and the fine arts of expression with philosophy and the sciences. For they also are an intrinsic part of the growth of the human spirit, of its feeling, its intuition; part, indeed, of the whole nature of man. To be sure, the whole nature of man, including reason, may exercise itself in battles. But in them there is more physical fact and violence than in the growth of poetry and painting, or the sweeter modes of religion.

With such rather crude distinctions in mind, I introduce the word "history." As applied to modes of human growth — science, philosophy, religion, and art — I regard their history as identical with the stages of their past which is projecting itself into the present. This is one of the two current meanings of the term. For "history" is taken sometimes as descriptive narrative and sometimes as the subject-matter itself in its evolving course and processes. Both senses of the word exist, whatever be the topic. Thus the "history" of the earth may be either the narrative called geology, or may be the very changes which geology is attempting to describe. And a "history" of mankind may be the narrative or, on the other hand, the very actual series of poignant human facts which follow on throughout the ages. In this sense the history of mankind would be mankind itself coming gradually to its present state; or the history of institutions would be the institutions themselves in the course of their growth; and, of course, the history of art or science would be art or science in its checkered course.

Clearly enough, if history, taken as narrative, is to be a thing of life and truth it must embody the verity, or veritable history, of the past; that is, must keep itself vitally one with the unfolding subject-matter which it is presenting. And it should absorb and re-express the elements of power moving the drama of mankind.

But a narrative composition is itself an event. It is part of the substance of its age, part of the intellectual conditions (which are actualities) of the time of its composition. The mind of Thucydides and the history which he wrote were elements of the period of the Peloponnesian War. So the sardonic Roman temper of Tacitus and the histories he composed were part of his epoch. Obviously

A LAYMAN'S VIEW OF HISTORY

contemporary documents and state papers are part of the event which they record. But Gibbon's *Decline and Fall* was one of the events of the eighteenth century, and part of the linkage between that century's consciousness of itself and its understanding of the past. We may speak in the same way of Mommsen's very Prussian *History of Rome*.

More brilliant examples of things which are events and also narratives are the works of imaginative literature and the figurative arts. They too are records and also profoundly part of the substance of events. The *Iliad* or the *Divina Commedia* is a concrete manifestation, a supreme expression, of the qualities of an epoch. On the other hand, if these poems are not what are called historical narratives, they are records and masses of evidence. So the Parthenon, or Chartres Cathedral, is a document, a piece of evidence, even a vehicle of narrative. But each of these temples is also a concrete and monumental embodiment of the skill, the resources and capacities, and the intellectual and spiritual qualities of an epoch.

So the works of Plato and Aquinas are demonstrative evidence of the Greek and medieval minds. They are also part of the substance of their respective epochs just as truly as the Battle of Plataea or the Babylonian captivity of the Holy See.

For the purpose of this address, I am taking "history" in the more vital sense of the very life and actuality of the past, out of which the present has arisen. And the two points which I have endeavored to bring out are, first, the oneness between the present and the past, and, secondly, the view of "history" as this very living past and present which, as narrative, it seeks to bring to a descriptive statement.

There is a further point of view which seems proper for us. We are historians and scholars, and I would say humanists, rather than physicists, mathematicians, or biologists. Whatever may be the view of our brethren the scientists, man is for us historians the centre of the world. We regard the sciences humanistically, as manifestations of the human mind and a phase of its growth. We are not investigators of the substantial data of the sciences, nor judges of their hypothetical accuracy or possible falsity as descriptions of the world. We are concerned with science as one of the modes of advance of human thought. And we bear in mind that physical science, and each branch of it, is a unity and a whole, made of its present and its past; so that the history of any science is verily that science itself in its entirety and continuous course from its beginning to what it is now and hereafter shall come to be.

We take similar interest in philosophy, that method and mass of ultimate consideration of fact or verity. We would regard it in its totality, which is its unity, and consists in an age-long and necessary mode of thought.

Many of us believe that religion is from God; but for us as historians it is another mode of the flowering of the human spirit, yet rather in the way of intuition and immediate conviction than by the gray path of reason. For us the past and present of religion, in all its manifestations, is one, even as philosophy is one. And we would make and keep our history of religion a true expression of its manifold growth and being.

In the same way we would work as historians of those glories of the mind which come to us in the forms of poetry and imaginative prose, and in the forms of the visual arts. And similarly would we view all human institutions, social, political, and belligerent — for man is a warring animal. We consider them in their time-unity, and, in studying them, should hold their past as one with their latest manifestations. So we weave into their growing web the salient events — battles, dynastic changes, executions, famines, and noisy revolutions, through which they have wound their course.

If we seek a further and universal unification of our conceptions of these manifold courses of human growth, perhaps we shall find it in a conception of humanity, of human life, one in its fruitful past and pregnant present. Human life may well be held a universal and dynamic unity in its manifestations, past, present, and to come; though for our intellectual and classificatory convenience we divide it into branches.

And now, if our considerations are valid, it becomes clear in what spirit and with what thoughts in mind we should write and teach history. We should strive to maintain this twofold unity, that of the time-dimension of

A LAYMAN'S VIEW OF HISTORY

past and present, and the pervasive unity of human life through its divers manifestations in religion, philosophy, science, institutions, and conduct. We should teach and write history as the veritable mirror, the *alter ego*, of this vibrant whole and unity of human growth. No one can compass this universal story. But each of us may set forth what he has to teach so that all the facts shall be constituent, and each fact shall appear in its topical relationship and exhibit its causal bearing. The story, and every part of it, is a linked emergent growth; and the facts which possess the broadest rational and connective value will best show its succeeding stages. Through the choice of such cardinal and potent facts, perhaps we may be able to present our topic in its furthest truth — as a chord in the symphony of man.

An awful time-honored figure looms before us, demanding to be dealt with. Its name is "historical fact." Since our history, taught or written, is to be truthful, the very *alter ego* of the course of events, one must take pains to be accurate. There is no telling when some small accuracy may prove a luminous link in

A LAYMAN'S VIEW OF HISTORY

the causal sequence. But usually accuracy relates to details and circumstances rather than to the larger features of the story. How can one be accurate about the Battle of Salamis or the assassination of Julius Caesar? — even though one were a contemporary with access to the newspapers of the following day. One will look to them for obvious details, which buzz about the fact. As for the event in its more essential nature, the historian will have to construct it out of his best knowledge and intelligence. Using our points of data, we form a conclusion as to how the event must have taken place, or probably took place. This is what every historian does of necessity. When he has determined the details, he has the more arduous task of their joinder and interpretation. Insight and judgment apply to this process, rather than accuracy. The result must be largely a matter of wise inference.

There are still two further considerations touching the conception of "historical fact." One is the human equation, and the other the multiple significance of every so-called fact.

A LAYMAN'S VIEW OF HISTORY

Mark well the disturbing function of the human equation. Not merely is the fact's interpretation affected, in ways dependent on the interpreter's intelligence and bent of interest. But, beyond this, a molding and creative manifold of understanding enters and makes part of the fact itself. Caesar's death had different significance for each one of those Roman notables whose swords met in his body. It was differently intended, and also bore different results, according to the temperament, motives, and situation of each. Indeed it was for each a different fact. No fact can be in and of itself alone. Every fact comes to pass in its relationships and bearings, as well as in itself — if indeed there be any clearly marked and delimited *itself*. The causes of Caesar's death had worked up to it through the whole antecedent history of Rome — of mankind, if you will. More immediately it was brought about by the tempers and motives of the conspirators. Neither its causes, its manifold significance, nor its effects could be the same for an ethical intellectual like Brutus and for the sweaty mob about to take the air in Caesar's gardens beyond the Tiber.

A LAYMAN'S VIEW OF HISTORY

Not only a striking event like Caesar's death, but every incident in life is exhaustless in its bearings; and since its substance extends to its relationships and effects, a multiplicity of actuality as well as meaning is very part of it.

But, furthermore, the understanding of a fact by contemporaries is part of its bearing and effect, and so part of the fact itself. This would, of course, apply to divergent understandings of it. Accounts that differ may be equally justifiable and equally true. Each one may set forth a different phase. Divergent histories, contemporary or future, may be each a receptacle and true expression of some actuality. But such histories are also part of the bearing and result of the fact, and so a part of it. And this is the ground of the justifiability, and indeed of the transcendent unity, of history as narrative and as one and the same with the course of the events described. As the events form an organic continuum, so should the expression be.

There is still a last complexity — perplexity it may seem. The very notion of fact, and what the real fact is, has varied marvellously among men; and this too, with no conscious weighing of the metaphysics of the matter. The phenomena, for example, of what we call the physical or natural world have been very differently viewed. Ordinary people accept them for what they appear. But the old Greek philosophers sought to find beneath them a profounder and causally explanatory fact. Such was the water of Thales, the atoms of Democritus, or the substance of Aristotle, or, if you will, the Ideas of Plato. None of these was either visible or tangible. Each was rather an explanation, an hypothesis, an assumed fact thrust forward, or thrust under, to explain things as they appeared. The nuclei and electrons of our modernized atoms may be a fact of this character. The ether at all events is such an explanatory fact, or hypothesis; and comes and goes at the call of physical theory.

Again, physical facts may be accepted symbolically; regarded as symbols of the verity which they carry, or which indeed they *are*, to the rightly instructed mind. The Church Fathers of the fourth and fifth centuries were prone to regard the facts of nature as

A LAYMAN'S VIEW OF HISTORY

symbols of the spiritual verity which it was their function to shadow forth. And, for some philosophers of the Middle Ages, the natural world, both in its creation and as presented before their eyes, was a divinely ordered allegory. Its actual reality, which appearances merely shadowed forth, lay in its spiritual and saving import.

As for so-called historical events, the Church Fathers, and after them the medieval theologians, admitted rather grudgingly the literal truth of the Old Testament narratives. That was but "the letter that killeth." The profounder verity, the deeper fact, was the salvation prefigured in them. It was their saving prefigurative meaning, which held "the spirit that maketh to live."

Some of us moderns, our Wordsworth for example, would still tend to find the deeper reality in the lesson, the teaching, the spiritual import of Nature. And in philosophy our extreme idealists, from Bishop Berkeley on, can find no reality beyond our thought.

Many of us to-day who are neither given over to allegory nor idealists of Berkeley's type still hesitate before our choice of fact or truth. We are haunted by the faith that the surest and most veritable fact is that which our whole human nature, passionate, spiritual, and intellectual, might somehow conspire to substantiate. Fact may not be just as we see it, or scientifically observe it. And perhaps fact is not just as reason argues it. Assuredly it is not what impulse and emotional conviction would declare; our intuitions will not suffice. We crave the concurrent verdict — if we could only get it — of all the faculties of our cognitive and assertive selves.

Thus I have tried to set before you a layman's view, in which history shall not be mere narrative, nor merely the series of events forming the past; but shall incorporate and be the onward-striding thought, the interwoven tissue of event itself, the element of continuity without which nothing is or can ever have been. Every object in nature, every bit of science, every philosophic theory, every phase and kind of religion, and every constructive or destructive act of life, possesses the constituent of being and becoming which is time. And the history of politics, of science, of philosophy, of art, or of religion, is politics, science, philos-

A LAYMAN'S VIEW OF HISTORY

ophy, art, or religion in its genesis, its emergent growth, its present, or even future, culmination and decay, through which its elements pass into other phases of the cosmic process.

OLD AGE

Old age is a time of valuations. There is scant activity to look forward to, but everything to consider that has made and still makes one's life. Since an old man's weakening powers are not likely to reach new truth, his thought may center in the happiness which lies in acceptance, serenity and peace.

No one contemplates either himself or the world dispassionately. Temper and desire are never absent. Each time of life has its intuitions and convictions, and an old man should realize that his view of things is moulded by his heart's desire. Whether thinking of himself or the world, he may be sure that his mind is reflecting whatever he has been, as well as what he has at last become.

Usually I am happy, or ashamed of myself when I am not. Why should not a favorable old age be the happiest time of life? The old man's present is wrapped in a retrospect freed from the toil and anxiety attending the strivings of his stronger years. The vista glows

OLD AGE

as one looks back thankful and unembittered — never admitting that objects unattained made life a failure, since endeavour has its own sanction. Even blameworthy acts may win atonement when seen at last in full disclosure. Inaction would be dull had we our old energy. But it were folly now to seek "deeds of youth." The wish for such has left me, and the quiet hour is often vivid with sudden images of things, like the canvases of old masters seen long ago indelibly.

Seek the present in the past and the past in the present. The world is always springing from a coöperating past and fashioning a future. The present is no severed cross-section. Nor is a man's past a clear-cut trail; its margins lose themselves in the surrounding world. What has not had a share in making us ourselves? Conversely every incident and act of our direct past has its ever widening repercussions. Judgment upon one's own life, past and present, must tally with our judgment of the world. But in the world's effect upon us, and ours on it, there are degrees of immediacy. I see my life as a streak of energy making its way amid influ-

A LAYMAN'S VIEW OF HISTORY

ences, some obvious and immediate, others greying off into the obscure. An enduring individual is seen, partly guiding himself and choosing from among his contacts; he seems to grow from within as well as through what comes to him. Circumstances aided his growth, or were somehow made to contribute.

But how did they come to favor, or were made to favor, him? Was it chance or the interworking of purposeless forces? Or were circumstances ordered so as to minister to my good? I cannot solve the world's riddle. But there is in me a conviction, a feeling, a faith. Fitfully, unsteadily, yet with recurring emotion, from boyhood I have held to a divine purpose through the world and extending to mankind. My own life, escaping various pitfalls, seems to have fulfilled itself happily. I am grateful for every bit of it, even for its broken hours; for I cannot but recognize the care and leading of God. I believe that He made me a vessel of His love, and gave me such a mind that I should turn to Him in gratitude and love. He surrounded me with vessels of His love — parents and relatives, friends deeply cared for and caring, and a beloved wife. He endowed me with a discerning intelligence; an understanding that should discriminate and choose from life's welter, and form a desire for the best. My will strengthened, and my purpose cleared, to accomplish the best that in me lay. My work became a loving labor. I may have steered my life with care, but how slight is one's power to shape a prosperous course. Fatalities may overtake one, happening through sheer chance so far as regards one's own foresight or control. My belief is that God cast the circumstances of my life, and led me happily on, that I might love Him and be a vessel of His love for others.[1]

It does not agree with the language of our *intelligentsia* to call oneself a vessel of God's love. But why not? According to the phi-

---

[1] A thoughtful person who accepts the idea of divine love must think it out for himself. The thought goes back to Plato and the Old Testament. I look at it in this way: God loves the world as one who makes something and tries to make it as good as possible. Thus God's love co-extends with his creativeness and includes beneficence. We find the climax of his creation in beings made as free as a finite creature can be. This creature, man, may respond to God's love and try to do God's will. If so, God's love flows on through him. But if he repels God's love or brutishly ignores it, he renounces his participation in the creative scheme, of which he cannot but form a part. Mortality — germination, birth, maturity, decay and passing — runs through all life. It is God's ceaseless renewal and refreshening of his creation.

losophy which I and countless others have held, no creature is outside God's purpose or can be other than a vessel of his will. There is something comic in the notion that religion and philosophy have been scrapped, while a scientific attitude has come to stay, as if men were never to weary of it. Some day it may appear that physics and chemistry merely disclose the ways and means of the divine purpose. To me, everything seems to play a part in the fulfilment of it. The bit of alga, the stalk of wheat, the oak, bacteria, insects, the larger animals advance it, both when functioning as organisms and when their substance or processes enter other combinations. So with men. The most rapacious, willy nilly, conform to it; then the ordinary givers and takers; and finally such as intend to act for the furtherance of good. Only the last may be conscious of wishing to further the divine intent. I have never doubted the efficiency of the divine purpose. I would be at one with God, not in the sense of even the most diaphanous or ghostly mingling, but by trying to will as He wills. His will seems to me a will toward coördination and, for mankind, mutual help-

OLD AGE

fulness with due regard for individual growth. Nature is an organization. Its innumerable ingredients are linked and rooted in each other, and all are elements and working factors of a self-sustaining world. Though they destroy each other, they willy-nilly give themselves each to all. The world has not burst suddenly into divine fulfilment. But I must think it endowed with power of growth — as living and evolving life. If this is a conclusion of faith, it is borne out by my intelligence and seems to agree with my experience. For the progression of organisms stands out from the geologic and paleontological record, and is evident in the present world of plants and animals.

Much of my life has been passed in studying the growth and passage of ideas from man to man, from people to people, and from age to age. It has been a noble task. Lately I have been re-reading history with my mind set on the acts of men, their governments or no-governments, their wars and rapine, the whole unspeakable oppression and destruction of man by man. I stand aghast. Yet looking downward from the remote past to our present,

I find amelioration. Violent and selfish as men show themselves, there is much devoted conduct, and mankind has grown less brutal. So an aged historian may console himself with a belief in progress or some sort of increase in the nobler elements of life. Here every argument is beset with incalculables and indefinables. It shapes itself in my mind somewhat thus : —

On this fifteenth of the great month of May in my old Connecticut home, the day glows with warmth and sun, and I am transported by the passion of life about me. Leaves grow large, flowers open, birds rush about or sing madly. The power of life bursts into myriad fulfilments. Impulse, rather than articulate purpose, stirs its surge. Nowhere is there intellectuality or thought, but the joy of living. Life reaches heights in many ways. One height is passionate love in its acme of fulfilment ; another is strong and steady affection. Violent action, possibly with rage, may be another, and another is intensive purposeful effort, through which thought wins to the goal of happiness.

The energy of life remains the source of

those aspiring modes which have become self-conscious, thoughtful and purposive. But that which has variety and value in thought cannot ignore the needs and impulses of the body. Pleasures of the senses have place with spiritual activities. The evolution of organisms is a joint growth of body and mind; but the psychic side of life becomes more and more directive. The goal lies in the full development of the mind of man and of such bodily faculties as enable it to act. This holds whether we think of mind and body as distinct or as different phases of a psycho-body. In the one case it would be mind, in the other the psychic phase, that emerges as the dominant agency of the impulse to satisfy human cravings.

The evolution resulting in *homo sapiens* may be viewed as accumulation of experience, which becomes tendency and turns to faculty. A huge part of the experience has been of the body, and in connection with the body all that we know of the activity of mind takes place. The primitive workings of mind mingle with bodily cravings and shrinkings. Only thousands of years of discipline enable man to select

A LAYMAN'S VIEW OF HISTORY

the ideas that will prove valid through agreement with the mass-convictions of prior experience. Early impressions pass from consciousness, but endure in the nature affected by them. The mind has no recollection of these submerged effects, which may still be at the bottom of irrational impulses and shudderings. Part of the mind's office is to bring all elements of human nature, including these unremembered but still effective crudities, into peaceful coördination with what is rationally approved.

Mind follows or checks its impulses and seeks to carry out its purposes, using the body or in conjunction with it. The result attained is more adventitious than the purpose and the effort to carry it out. The most distinctively human side of mankind's progress consists in the evolution of impulse and feeling and intuition, of thought and purpose, of energy and tenacity of effort.

But what sort of impulse, what manner of thought and purpose? For impulse the criterion would lie in its relatedness to the man's whole nature; for thought, in its comprehensiveness; for purpose, in its strength and steadiness. Obviously the impulse should not

OLD AGE

be one of transient violence due to some accidental stimulus, and out of accord with the sum of impulses and tendencies making up character. The thought should be all-considering, and the purpose in such broad accord with the man's potential growth that the effort to realize it may form the unifying energy of his life.

The impulse to live is manifest in the struggle between the insistences of the individual — the inclusive impulse and desire to enhance his life and be himself grandiloquently — and the demands of others. The tide of human progress floods and ebbs within the range of this conflict and the endeavor to adjust it. It is the creator and destroyer of custom and institution. It makes and alters family relationships, and builds the fabric of the social order, with its kingships, aristocracies, democracies, its armies and its fleets. It is always with us, its phases multiplying with the growing complexity of human relations. Human progress lies in turning it from violence to discussion and persuasion.

Some modes of effort and attainment do not spring from this conflict directly, though they have kinship with it from the nature of all human striving. Even though unconnected with this conflict, action involves choice and an adjustment of desires, as in the thinking of a philosopher or the investigations of a physicist. Yet the physicist might be engaged on the improvement of cannon, and the discussion in Plato's *Republic* has to do with the conflict I am speaking of. So art and poetry and religion may create within or without its bounds. The choice inherent in all endeavor harks back to the Heraclitean word, "strife is the lord of all." Strife or striving, the aim and the effort to reach it, are the human part of all that has come to man or been attained by him.

Any review of the succession of generations and peoples is limited to what can be seen. Who can appraise the total coördinated effect of the anterior world? A student can consider only those portions of the past which come within his ken, and he may do well to focus his mind upon the lines of antecedents which seem to converge causally upon a period and to enter it as factors. He will see that each present, in virtue of its capacities and limi-

OLD AGE

tations, receives and uses or absorbs some elements, and not others which once were strong. A present carves out its past. It takes what its capacities permit, and refashions its heritage or spoil into congruity with itself. Periods commonly regarded as progressive take from the past whatever agrees with the character of their progress, and this may be what is most worthy to be handed on. But epochs of prevailing decay and dissolution are apt to select and transmit the weaker and more senseless parts of their inheritance.[1]

It is hard to distinguish an individual's faculties from the experience that disciplines and becomes part of them. The experience of a people also becomes part of its faculties or nature. Again, as an individual has no complete and unchanging memory of his youth, but keeps remembering incidents in

[1] A good example is the reception by the progressive fifteenth and sixteenth centuries in Italy, France and England of the classical heritage of art and literature, philosophy and science; while an opposite instance is Isidore of Seville in the sixth century selecting from the works of Augustine the most foolish notions of the great church thinker. Or finally, for a composite example, not till the Middle Ages had themselves notably advanced, did they "discover" and accept the Pandects of Justinian. They had used till then such crude epitomes of Roman law as were sufficient for their needs and suited to their rude intelligence.

conformity with the emphasis of his maturity, so a people remembers and accepts what it can assimilate and use. Finally, although an individual's past has grown into his present, nevertheless it is always his living self that creates and acts. So any present time, with all its inworking past, is still itself, and its energies and temperament produce whatever it brings forth, including what it is making out of its past. Absorbing its past, it becomes itself. There is no break; the still efficient past and the living present are a continuum of experience and action. This does not imply the complete determination of successive epochs by their pasts. The present has predilections, and exerts choice, insists on being what it will. Two notions should be avoided when reviewing either individual lives or the history of mankind; one is the notion of complete determination, the other that of unfailing freedom of choice and will. There are always determining factors and always some freedom.

Our continuum shows no constant progress, no unbroken increase or betterment of life. There come periods of decay, when much seems to perish. Weakness and blight recur and, sometimes, overthrow. The whole world is never in the same stage. There is incompatibility, even hostility, in contacts between peoples or cultures. There is never full adjustment of individual insistences and social needs or of divergent class interests. Convention is incomplete; customs fail to hold; violence is never quite superceded by persuasion. And as with individuals, so with peoples, strenuous effort is followed by fatigue and lapse of energy.

No historian can number the elements of progress any more than he can analyze life. And however impartially he would distinguish what is of value, he cannot escape the pull of his own tastes. His approvals and strictures chime with his nature. He accepts what he cares for, and is jarred by what he dislikes. Fields of neutral data may be scarcely noticed, and vast ranges of life's incidents, impacts, and shadowy touches remain beyond his ken. While reconstructing the past, his mind is drawn to what moves his own epoch and, above all, to what has entered into him. The fulcrum of attention is himself; his interest focusses on the past of his own thought. To me the historic world presents a vista of emotional urge, spiritual growth, intellectual achievement — flowerings of the spirit in feeling, consideration, insight, comprehensiveness of thought. From the beginning, work fundamental necessities, the need of custom, of convention, of organization. They inhere in all social life, and produce the efficient forms of its advance. The oldest peoples are helpful in the family and show forbearances beyond it. Each human group is a phase of social maintenance, of adjustment of individual and class insistences. From the beginning also I discern the need of force to check promiscuous violence and meet crises within or from without. No society, no self-glorious nation, has reached a state of complete reasonableness or has been quite safe from attack. There must be police and a fighting force ever more elaborately organized and equipped as nations advance in industry and civilization.

When viewing the rise of decent and comfortable living, I perceive a radiation of noble qualities. These may follow upon stable ways of life, or may come before, as with Homer's splendid creatures. Barbarous the settings of their lives, but vibrant their energies and beautiful their thoughts. They far outshine the Babylonians, who were bedded in comfort some millenniums before Homer sang. Trade and agriculture flourished in Babylonia; there was police, an army, a well-equipped monarchy, a code of laws, a knowledge of the stars. But no such marvel of a man as Odysseus lived in Mesopotamia, or in Ancient Egypt, where life was easy for the rich, where ethics were becoming benevolent, and religion rose above the fear-stricken demonology of Babylon. Fine artisans and artists were the Egyptians, but poor in logic and the curiosity which leads men on.

All ancient peoples had some desire to know; but the intellectual life opens with the Greeks. They drew knowledge from the East as well as Egypt. Their borrowings spurred their minds. Greatest of individualists, they excelled in the energy of will to have whatever might enrich their lives. They reasoned on man's good and ill; discussed the conduct of the individual, the conduct of the city. They were not constant in civic self-control, however admirably they proved that the city was above the individual. A Greek was rarely moved by broad Hellenic devotion, and might be a factious citizen. Yet he was absorbed in his city. Family life was meagre; he did little more than sleep in his small comfortless dwelling. He lived in the public places of the city, which he adorned with buildings, symbols of its mind and power. City politics were the fruit of passionate desire, of vivid thought and eager action. The citizens led self-determined lives within the laws, rather than under them. They might give themselves to the city's defence or its ambitions, or be busied with gain. There were buildings to be erected and statues to be made. Fame could be won from tragedies or biting comedies, and gain, too, from odes glorifying generous patrons. Histories were to be composed and governments studied or nature's phenomena; the genesis of the cosmos was rationally discussed, as well as the mind's knowledge of the good.

Such expressions of the Greek pursuit of life drew together in a common insistence upon fitness, proportion, and a true correlation of thought with conduct, — qualities exemplified

OLD AGE

in epic, lyric, and dramatic poetry, in sculpture and architecture. Their presence in whatever, through these means, was presented to the mind and mood, constituted beauty.

The efforts of the Greek genius were an unfolding of human life. The Roman contribution sprang from stanchness in civic devotion and a genius for political and military organization and for civil law. Self-control preserved an adjustment of individual volition to the needs of the Republic. The Roman felt few personal allures. He lacked imaginative desire, and had but a dull sense of beauty. He was citizen and *pater familias*. Tenacity of purpose, indomitable will, pushed on the Roman Republic to Mediterranean domination. The Greek enlightenment made it conscious of an imperial destiny.

Tu regere imperio populos, Romane, memento;
Hae tibi erunt artes, pacisque imponere morem,
Parcere subjectis, et debellare superbos.

This idea did not spring from the provincial Roman mind, nor from the Greek city-states. But it inhered in the deeds and plans of Alexander; and the leaven of Greek thought caused it to flower and bear fruit in the Rome of Virgil and Augustus.

The Roman Empire brought to the Mediterranean world peace and the persuasive reason of Greco-Roman civilization. A new cosmopolitanism was evolved; hard-bitten nationalities relaxed; men's minds and moods were opened to alien opinions and became sensitive to the influence of natures different from their own. Diffusion of ideas and cross-fertilization of thought took place, while that which in an earlier century might have remained a local Galilean faith, spread from east to west. Greek thinking and the genius of the Empire refashioned the new religion, made it acceptable, and gave it an organizing energy which was not in Jesus or in Paul. Neither the unalloyed teachings of the one nor the unmitigated doctrines of the other could have become a world-religion functioning in a universal church.

Greek thought, Roman order and the Christian Church struggled against the impact of barbarism from without and institutional decay within. But the Empire succumbed. The old bottles of Greek and Roman civilization did not suit the thought and feeling of the Christian Middle Ages. In the transitional and early mediaeval centuries the forms of civilization fell back — literature, the arts and crafts, political and social competence, the comforts and decencies of life. With enough to do to fend for themselves, men had no surplus mental ardor. The studious were toilsomely rearranging and flattening to their duller apprehensions the theme of salvation set forth by the Church Fathers; they were salvaging, at the same time, the rudiments of secular education. The ripening Middle Ages took these matters and recast them. Emotion cleared itself through expression, and the mind regained effective unity. Then were created fitting forms of mediaeval thinking, new themes of poetry and life, and a cathedral architecture answering religious aspiration; a measure of classic truth and beauty was regained, and the great Digest of Justinian studied and made use of.

Somewhat squalid in externalities, precious in their inner life, the Middle Ages meditated upon divine and human governance, opened new vistas of piety as well as mortal love, thus contributing to human growth and human yearning. In the succeeding centuries of humanism and reform the ways of progress gained in volume and complexity. From the fourteenth century onward, the increase of wealth and comfort takes different forms in Italy and France, England and Germany. There was splendor and luxury in Italy; in the north the merchants of the towns grew rich and built statelier houses, while the lots of workers in town and country followed slowly. Consolidation of territorial oppression into royal tyrannies brought some lessening of violence. Under the expansion of mental energy, the desires and predilections of the time moved in two circuits, interrelated and overlapping. They might be called pagan and Christian: — the lures and lusts of life, as opposed to the soul's salvation in the glory of God; also science, natural knowledge and discovery, with a new philosophy: over against this a truculent if not radical reconsideration of the sanctions of faith and the authority of the Church.

With the sixteenth century, ideals of feeling, imagination and intellect came to clear and noble expression in language and in pictorial and plastic art. All that the time had absorbed from the past, all that its own insight saw, the many things it prized and reasoned on and grasped at, were set forth in forms that were magnificent creations. With no notable originality of thought, the power of expression developed the qualities of the period and uplifted its ideals. A glorious presentation of the unattainable in life and conduct set before wistful humanity a conceptual reality which drew men on to efforts beyond their normal scope.

An illustration through contrast may be found in the term *bourgeois*, which implies the limitation of effort to the obviously possible and a resulting contraction of human genius and endeavour. It has no place for adventure, and in the sixteenth century adventure was opening shores across the sea, and even merchants were "merchant adventurers." The seraphs of expression, Michelangelo and Rafael, Marlowe and Shakespeare, were not bourgeois. They lifted adventure to regions of the spirit, and gave it forms that lured men on to strive beyond themselves.

A LAYMAN'S VIEW OF HISTORY

So the sixteenth century promoted life and offered patterns for its future advance, through an expression of ideals and possibilities in painting, poetry and drama, as well as in the philosophy of Francis Bacon, so vast and stimulating and unworkable. Perfect form and phrase partly explains the tempering effect of the French Montaigne and the English *Book of Common Prayer*, as well as the potency of Luther and Calvin.[1] The seventeenth century follows, great likewise in expression and more creative in thought. Shakespeare was still writing plays at the beginning, and Milton came magnificent in verse and mighty in polemics. Racine and Molière present the zenith of French poetry and drama, while Pascal with one side of his mind casts in immortal phrases a pietistic contemplation of man and his world, and with the other pushes forward the science of physics. Descartes opens new fields of mathematics, and resets the foundations of philosophy, on which Spinoza shall build and Leibnitz. The *Method* and the *Ethics* were also achievements in ex-

[1] Cf. the concluding chapter in my *Thought and Expression in the Sixteenth Century*.

OLD AGE

pression; and Newton's laws, which remodelled men's thoughts of the moving heavens, were formulas, symbols or castings together of knowledge into statement, and so grandiose expressions.

If the eighteenth and nineteenth centuries have no such expressional peaks, they advance in science and philosophy, in industrial production, in struggles with social problems, and in anxious consciousness of the disparity of human lots. With life more comfortable for the well-to-do, and physical pain less common, came a quicker realization of others' sufferings, and the ills that had seemed matter of course became intolerable. Prisons improved and asylums for the insane. Anaesthetics in surgery was a civilizing influence. Man continued a fighting animal, and wars were evil as ever; but, in peace, life was less brutal, more civilized. All this promoted thought, which is apt to be less active under squalid conditions. The rapidly increasing efficiency of machines displaced, and still displaces, human labor, threatening the laborer's maintenance and lowering his skill and adaptability. Yet production and living may adjust themselves.

A LAYMAN'S VIEW OF HISTORY

The universe remains a debatable mystery, and so does life. But knowledge of nature has grown enormously, and with it the cure and prevention of disease. Assuredly here is progress, though the ethical or social control of man's heightened power has not kept pace. Much human conduct — like the Great War — springs demon-like from inheritances of passion and violence; but our present humiliated consciousness may carry good. Though this stumbling world is sorely troubled in this year of grace 1935, there is some justification for an old man's faith in the meaning of it all. My faith reflects the intent and course of my own life. It finds a world moving on pursuant to divine purpose, and gladdens me as I look forward to passing into the Great Mother whose myriad issue somehow reflects the mind of God. The individual seems ill fitted for eternity; there is little of myself that I would keep intact. I have had a goodly life, mind working to the full, love evoked, stricken for its own good, at last fulfilled. What further could one wish? Human relations are drenched with mortality. Grateful to God, I would fare on in an ever deepening peace.

"THE EDUCATION OF HENRY ADAMS"

I

Little will be said of Henry Adams that he would not have deprecated. It is not easy to avoid misinterpretation and perversity of speech touching one who was always puzzling over life, and presenting himself, as well as the Universe, for a puzzle to his friends. Perhaps he was less of an enigma to his nieces, by blood or adoption, upon whom in his latter years he leaned so charmingly for sympathy and care. He confided in the wisdom of women, generalizing from an elder sister's happy adjustment of a plan of travel in his youth: "It was his first experiment in giving the reins to a woman, and he was so much pleased with the results that he never wanted to take them back. In after life he made a general law of experience — no woman had ever driven him wrong, no man had ever driven him right."

The same whimsical admiration seems to inspire his delightful appreciation of the Vir-

A LAYMAN'S VIEW OF HISTORY

gin's rôle in medieval culture presented in his *Mont St. Michel and Chartres*, and is returned to, *con amore*, in the volume giving the title to this article. But mere man, though he feel the affection of an old pupil, must at least be honest when writing about Mr. Adams; for no member of the Adams family could endure a dishonest word spoken of him, or even of the way in which he may have posed before himself and the world.

Perhaps no other American has left such a mass of clever writing, evolved through a life of thoughtful research and curious reflection, and has died so unrecognized by the public, educated or otherwise. It was not long after the death of his brother Charles Francis, that Henry Adams said to me at his home in Washington, "The cab-drivers point out this house as the residence of the late Charles Francis Adams!"[1]

Is it because the serious study of American history — other than local — has so few votaries that such a work as Henry Adams's nine-volumed *History of the United States, 1807–*

---

[1] It should be remembered that this article was written in 1918, the year of Henry Adams's death. Since then prodigious recognition has come to him.

1817, with its ancillary lives of *Albert Gallatin* and *John Randolph*, and publication of *Documents*, should have drawn so small attention to the writer? And to one who had written admirably in the reviews, and had edited the *North American*? At all events, with the publication of these works, he abandoned the political history of the United States for the more succulent æsthetic and human values recoverable from the European Middle Ages. But Mr. Adams no longer "published": he merely "printed," in order to obtain, as he said, the criticism of his friends upon the *Mont St. Michel* and the *Education*. He made no effort to be read. Did he care? He says not, in a letter: "I am satisfied that it is immaterial whether one man or a thousand or a hundred thousand read one's books. The author is as safe as the seventeenth-century clergyman who printed his Sermon on Righteousness."

A born "intellectual," Henry Adams was a virtuoso in writing, caring always for form, and possessing an inborn or sedulously acquired aptitude for the phrase and for the artistic and effective paragraph. There is little more perfect in American literature than the opening chapter of the *Education*, telling of his childhood's summers passed in Quincy at his grandfather's, who did not die till Henry was ten years old.

The house was on the hill . . . with a far view eastward over Quincy Bay, and northward over Boston. Till his twelfth year, the child passed his summers there, and his pleasures of childhood mostly centred in it. Of education he had as yet little to complain. Country schools were not very serious. Nothing stuck to the mind except home impressions, and the sharpest were those of kindred children; but as influences that warped a mind, none compared with the mere effect of the back of the President's bald head, as he sat in his pew on Sundays, in line with that of President Quincy, who, though some ten years younger, seemed to children about the same age. Before railways entered the New England town, every parish church showed half-a-dozen of these leading citizens, with gray hair, who sat on the main aisle in the best pews, and had sat there, or in some equivalent dignity, since the time of St. Augustine, if not since the glacial epoch. It was unusual for boys to sit behind a President grandfather, and to read over his head the tablet in memory of a President great-grandfather, who had 'pledged his life, his fortune, and his sacred honor' to secure the independence of his country, and so forth; but boys naturally supposed, without much reasoning, that other boys had the equivalent of President grandfathers, and that churches would always go on, with the baldheaded leading citizens on the main aisle, and Presidents or their equivalents on the walls. The Irish gardener once said to the child: 'You'll be thinkin' you'll be President too!' The casuality of the remark made so strong an impression on his mind that he never forgot it. He could not remember ever to have thought on the subject; to him, that there should be a doubt of his being President was a new idea. What had been would continue to be. He doubted neither about Presidents nor about Churches, and no one suggested at that time a doubt whether a system of society which had lasted since Adam would outlast one Adams more.

The portrait of his grandmother is a marvel of finesse and tenderness:—

The Madam was a little more remote than the President, but more decorative. She stayed much in her own room with the Dutch tiles, looking out on her garden with the box walks, and seemed a fragile creature to a boy who sometimes brought her a note or a message, and took distinct pleasure in looking at her delicate face under what seemed to him very becoming caps. He liked her refined figure; her gentle voice and manner; her vague effect of not belonging there, but to Washington or to Europe, like her furniture, and writing-desk with little glass doors above and little eighteenth-century volumes in old binding, labelled Peregrine Pickle or Tom Jones or Hannah More.

Try as she might, the Madam could never be Bostonian, and it was her cross in life, but to the boy it was her charm. Even at that age, he felt drawn to it. The Madam's life had been in truth far from Boston. She was born in London in 1775, daughter of Joshua Johnson, an American merchant, brother of Governor Thomas Johnson of Maryland, and Catherine Nuth, of an English family in London. Driven from England by the revolutionary war, Joshua Johnson took his family to Nantes, where they remained till the peace. The girl Louisa Catherine was nearly ten years old when brought back to London, and her sense of nationality must have been confused; but the influence of the Johnsons and the services of Joshua obtained for him from President Washington the appointment of Consul in London on the organization of the government in 1790.

In 1794 President Washington appointed John Quincy Adams minister to the Hague. He was twenty-seven years old when he returned to London and found the Consul's house a very agreeable haunt. Louisa was then twenty.

At that time, and long afterwards, the Consul's house, far more than the Minister's, was the centre of contact for travelling Americans, either official or other. The Legation was a shifting point, between 1785 and 1815; but the Consulate, far down in the City, near the Tower, was convenient and inviting; so inviting that it proved fatal to young Adams. Louisa was charming, like a Romney portrait, but among her many charms that of being a New England woman was not one. The defect was serious. Her future mother-in-law, Abigail, a famous New England woman whose authority over her turbulent husband, the second President, was hardly so great as that which she exercised over her son, the sixth to be, was troubled by the fear that Louisa might not be made of stuff stern enough, or brought up in conditions severe enough, to suit a New England climate, or to make an efficient wife for her paragon son, and Abigail was right on that point, as on most others where sound judgment was involved; but sound judgment is sometimes a source of weakness rather than of force, and John Quincy already had reason to think that his mother held sound judgments on the subject of daughters-in-law, which human nature, since the fall of Eve, made Adams helpless to realise.

Being three thousand miles away from his mother, and equally far in love, he married Louisa in London, July 26, 1797, and took her to Berlin to be the head of the United States Legation. During three or four exciting years, the young bride lived in Berlin; whether she was happy or not, whether she was content or not, whether she was socially successful or not, her descendants did not surely know; but in any case she could by no chance have become educated there for a life in Quincy or Boston.

In 1801 the overthrow of the Federalist party drove her and her husband to America, and she became at last a member of the Quincy household; but by that time her children needed all her attention, and she remained there, with occasional winters in Boston and Washington, till 1809. Her husband was made Senator in 1803, and in 1809 was appointed Minister to Russia. She went with him to St. Petersburg, taking her baby, Charles Francis, born in 1807; but broken-hearted at having to leave her two older boys behind. The life at St. Petersburg was hardly gay for her; they were far too poor to shine in that extravagant society; but she survived it, though her little girl baby did not, and in the winter of 1814-15, alone with the boy of seven years old, crossed Europe from St. Petersburg to Paris, in her travelling-carriage, passing through the armies, and reaching Paris in the *Cent Jours* after Napoleon's return from Elba. Her husband next went to England as Minister, and she was for two years at the Court of the Regent.

In 1817 her husband came home to be Secretary of State, and she lived for eight years in F Street, doing her work of entertainer for President Monroe's administration. Next she lived four miserable years in the White House. When that chapter was closed in 1829, she had earned the right to be tired and delicate, but she still had fifteen years to serve as wife of a Member of the House, after her husband went back to Congress in 1833. Then it was that the little Henry, her grandson, first remembered her, from 1843 to 1848, sitting in her panelled room, at breakfast, with her heavy silver tea-pot and sugar-bowl and cream-jug, which came afterwards to him and still exist somewhere as an heirloom of the modern safety-vault. By that time she was seventy years old or more, and thoroughly weary of being beaten about a stormy world. To the boy she seemed singularly peaceful, a vision of silver gray, presiding over her old President and her Queen Anne mahogany; an exotic, like her Sèvres china; an object of deference to every one, and of great affection to her son Charles; but hardly more Bostonian than she had been fifty years before, on her wedding-day, in the shadow of the Tower of London.

This portrait of an exquisite grandmother is a parallel to the writer's appreciation of the medieval Virgin. There was never a touch of cynicism or disillusionment in anything he had to say of symbolical or dead women, any more than in his conversation with their living daughters. Men were less convincingly admirable; yet penetrating and subtle sketches of men follow through this book, surpassing in charm and psychological quality those which make the oases in Lord Morley's recent volumes of *Reminiscences*. The elucidation of the character and mentality of his father, Charles Francis Adams, Senior, is very careful and quite different from the characterization of him in the writings of another son, Charles Francis. Henry writes : —

His father's character was therefore the larger part of his education, as far as any single person affected it, and for that reason, if for no other, the son was always a much interested critic of his father's mind and temper. Long after his death as an old man of eighty, his sons continued to discuss this subject with a good deal of difference in their points of view. To his son Henry, the quality that distinguished his father from all the other figures in the family group, was that, in his opinion, Charles Francis Adams possessed the only perfectly balanced mind that ever existed in the name. For a hundred years, every newspaper scribbler had, with more or less obvious excuse, derided or abused the older Adamses for their want of judgment. They abused Charles Francis for his judgment. Naturally they never attempted to assign values to either; that was the children's affair; but the traits were real. Charles Francis Adams was singular for mental poise, — absence of self-assertion or self-consciousness, — the faculty of standing apart without seeming aware that he was alone, — a balance of mind and temper that neither challenged nor avoided notice, nor admitted question of superiority or inferiority, of jealousy, of personal motives, from any source, even under great pressure. This unusual poise of judgment and temper, ripened by age, became the more striking to his son Henry as he learned to measure the mental faculties themselves, which were in no way exceptional either for depth or range. Charles Francis Adams's memory was hardly above the average; his mind was not bold like his grandfather's or restless like his father's, or imaginative or oratorical — still less mathematical; but it worked with singular perfection, admirable self-restraint, and instinctive mastery of form. Within its range it was a model.

II

Evidently the foil to his father's personality in Henry Adams's mind, was the more resplendent figure of Charles Sumner, the object of the youth's loving, but passing admiration.

A LAYMAN'S VIEW OF HISTORY

According to the analysis in the *Education*, Sumner's friendship for the elder C. F. Adams seems to have rather worse than tottered when President Lincoln, in April, 1861, appointed Adams Minister to England. Ignoring or ignorant of Sumner's disapproval, Mr. Adams accepted the appointment, and took with him his son Henry as private secretary. Years of preëminent service were now to follow, rendered by the father to his country, while for the son of twenty-three they made the chief obvious episode of a life. His impression of their events is given in a tense and dramatic narrative, which, as he protests, "is not a story of the diplomatic adventures of Charles Francis Adams, but of his son Henry's adventures in search of an education." Yet the temperamental presentation does but enhance the master-interest of the diplomatic parable.

It opens with humorous pathos, the minister on his voyage recalling how his grandfather had sailed in 1778 "on a diplomacy of adventure," taking his son John Quincy, then eleven years of age; how his father, that same John Quincy, again had sailed for Russia in 1809, with himself a baby, "almost as much of an adventurer as John Adams before him, and almost as successful. He thought it natural that the government should send him out as an adventurer also, with a twenty-three-year-old son."

This final private secretary had learned reticence, and not to grumble, by the time "the party landed at Liverpool, May 13, 1861, and went straight up to London: a family of early Christian martyrs about to be flung into an arena of lions, under the glad eyes of Tiberius Palmerston."

Lord Palmerston had arranged the ceremony, the immolation — consisting in the official announcement that England recognized the belligerency of the Confederacy. Whatever his father felt and concealed, the thud produced a dulness of comprehension in the son. He had all his thinking to reverse, and now must learn that nobody in England

doubted that Jefferson Davis had made or would make a nation, and nearly all were glad of it, though not often saying so. They mostly imitated Palmerston, who, according to Mr. Gladstone, 'desired the severance as a diminution of a dangerous power, but prudently held his tongue.' The sentiment of

A LAYMAN'S VIEW OF HISTORY

anti-slavery had disappeared. Lord John Russell, as Foreign Secretary, had received the rebel emissaries, and had decided to recognise their belligerency before the arrival of Mr. Adams, in order to fix the position of the British Government in advance. The recognition of independence would then become an understood policy; a matter of time and occasion.

It may be as well to remark here that the passage just quoted looks upon English sentiment from a London standpoint, and ignores the friendliness of other parts of England — of the Lancashire cotton-spinners for example, who, against their palpable interests and with ruin staring them in the face, upheld the Union cause. The private secretary stranded in London was not likely to learn of this. Officially obliged to go wherever his father or mother needed escort, the young man keenly felt his social isolation, which might also be some comfort to him as, at the end of his first season, "he hugged himself in his solitude when the story of the battle of Bull Run appeared in the *Times*." The minister's continuance in London seemed precarious enough. "For the next year they went on only from week to week, ready to leave England at once, and never assuming more than three months for their limit. Europe was waiting to see them go."

This was not to be. Even the affair of Mason and Slidell was weathered. The minister was lucky in his opponents — Mr. Mason for example. His own position in London gradually improved. At least he was not open to ridicule. Society took on the habit of accepting him, of treating him cordially "as, by birth and manners, one of themselves." Friends, strong and useful, began to show themselves — Monckton Milnes and William E. Forster, whose portraits are duly given. "Milnes was the good-nature of London; the Gargantuan type of its refinement and coarseness; the most universal figure of May Fair."

And then, those pillars of defense and engines of offense as well, John Bright and Richard Cobden. These last two "took bluntly the side of the Union against Palmerston, whom they hated. Strangers to London society, they were at home in the American Legation, delightful dinner-company, talking always with reckless freedom." They were friendly with the young man, who also began to make friends of his own. But he longed to break away — to go home!

"Of the year 1862 Henry Adams could never think without a shudder." There in London he did not hate the rebels: he hated the British government — its Palmerston, and its Lord John Russell, whose "form of defense," for example, in the matter of the sailing of the Alabama from Liverpool, "covered intent to kill." Through a mordant analysis of facts, the book shows the persistently hostile conduct of Lord John, scarcely veiled in an obliquity of statement, which Gladstone threw to the winds in his famous, subsequently apologized for, indiscretion of October 7, 1862.

Obviously Minister Adams had need of all his friends and all his collectedness to maintain himself in the face of hostile sentiment and unfriendly action. Very tense are these pages, through which may be traced the painful amelioration of the situation. We feel the anxiousness of the Minister's contention with Lord Palmerston and Lord John Russell, the stiffening of his support from Secretary Seward; we note the sending over of efficient Americans, like Thurlow Weed, to aid his efforts, the reaction within the British Cabinet, the resounding blows of Bright, the strengthening news of Vicksburg and Gettysburg — all of which enabled Minister Adams to win "the battle of the rams," and prevent the sailing, from the Lairds' yards at Birkenhead, of the two armored cruisers intended to break the blockade of the Southern coast. The crisis was past, and the four-years' tension of nerve relaxed.

III

Much could be quoted from these pages giving the turns of the diplomatic drama, and the diversions of the private secretary in the company of an increasing number of attractive friends. But the story of his further intellectual fortunes draws us on, the story of an Education, which the book professes to be.

The lessons of diplomacy had interjected queer disturbing elements into the vacuum of Bostonian adolescence. It was all unsatisfactory. The writer's frequent reiteration of his failure to get this education need not intrigue us; for the education which Henry

A LAYMAN'S VIEW OF HISTORY

Adams was to seek through experience of men and the reading of many books meant, not only personal enlightenment, but a rational explanation of the World. This becomes more evidently the theme of the latter half of the book, where nothing correspondingly concrete succeeds the exciting diplomatic narrative and the idyllic picture of a childhood. One may recall how the Voltairean wanderings of the second part of the *Roman de la Rose* follow the *precieux* but lovely idyl with which the poem opens.

Sir Charles Lyell was intimate at the Legation, and Henry, impelled by admiration for the great geologist, reviewed the new edition of Lyell's *Principles of Geology*, in an article for the *North American*. He became absorbed in Darwinism, which he professes not to have understood. Yet he drew the stimuli of its facts and inductions into his own perplexed thinking upon humanity. Perils attend the lay endeavor to read the concepts and principles of physical science into the lessons of human experience; they are bravely incurred by Mr. Adams. "At the very outset Adams struck on Sir Charles's Glacial Theory or theories. He was ignorant enough to think that the glacial epoch looked like a chasm between him and a uniformitarian world. If the glacial period was uniformity, what was catastrophe?" In later life Henry Adams was to become the close friend of another geologist, Clarence King, whose memory and *mots* are still green. He does not give in his *Education* the frivolous explanation of the Boston climate offered by his friend: "Boston was 1,387,453 years under the ice; and then the Adamses came."

It is well to remember that the mental progress or intellectual bafflings recorded here are given as they returned to the writer when he was an old man. Thus they came to him in retrospection when he was writing *The Education of Henry Adams: a Study of Twentieth Century Multiplicity*. He set them down as they appeared to him through the transforming distance, as he looked back upon his earlier self wandering through that faded labyrinth of fact and lucubration, seeking some light of universal, or at least rational, purpose. In the later time heart-breaking domestic affliction goaded him to the quest yet held too sad a barrier to his eyes. The real refuge was to be consideration, and whatever else is shadowed in that St. Gaudens statue in the Rock Hill Cemetery in Washington — at the foot of which now Henry Adams also lies.

But more tangible labors had actually filled out his life and ministered to its content. For Adams was a man of industry, always doing more work than he confessed to. With him all facts had to be inter-related into meaning and significance. "For facts as such I have a profound contempt," he said one day in his classroom; just as in his *Education* he remarks that, "nothing in education is so astonishing as the amount of ignorance it accumulates in the form of inert facts." He taught history at Harvard from 1870 to 1877, at the latter date intimating to me, disappointed of his teaching for my coming senior year, that he had been professor as long as one ought to be. He says in his book that he left with a sense of failure; but it certainly was far from that in the convictions of his students. He was the first teacher of history at Harvard to discard the textbook, and put his students to work for themselves.

Clarence King, John La Farge, and John Hay were the chief friends and outer luminaries of Mr. Adams's later life. They made a rare quartet.

Of all the men who had deeply affected their friends since 1850 John La Farge was certainly the foremost, and for Henry Adams, who had sat at his feet since 1872, the question how much he owed La Farge could be answered only by admitting that he had no standard to measure it by. Of all his friends La Farge alone owned a mind complex enough to contrast against the commonplaces of American uniformity.

Arcades ambo! No one ever thought of plumbing John La Farge, or Henry Adams either. But the former — artist always, and wonderful discourser — "repulsed argument." On a trip to the South Seas taken by the two together, La Farge in the warm Tahiti nights, would tell his companion, "Adams, you reason too much." One night, after an argument, La Farge dreamed that he was disturbed by the *mind* of Henry Adams rattling around the room. It turned out to be a rat. Apropos of this dream and of certain chapters in our book, we may say that the Universe is so big that one's mind is sure to rattle round it, unless thought encyst itself in some strayed fragment, which it can never quite correlate with the whole. Nearer the La Fargean vein is a bit of an old man's funny letter written by Mr. Adams in April two years go: —

DEAR INFANT . . . Yesterday I walked in the spring woods, and met a fly. To that fly I said: 'Fly! do you want me to tell you the truth about yourself?' And that fly winked at me — carefully — and said: 'You be damned.' — They have told me that just seventy-eight times. They are not tired, but I am.

But the latter part of the book does not lack a potent coherency, given it by the deft union of two connected themes, both of them prophetic of the present position and function of the United States. In 1884 Adams and his friend Hay built themselves adjoining houses on Lafayette Square in Washington, and spent there the greater part of the years still falling to them. Mr. Adams was always intimate with men who guided events in Washington, if not with the 'best-sellers' there. From these surroundings, but more distinctly from the vantage-ground of his own study and reflection, he lays before us the progressing grades of self-consciousness through which the United States came to recognize itself as a world-power and undertook to act accordingly. This theme weaves itself around an affectionate exposition — glorification, indeed — of the career of John Hay as Ambassador to England and afterwards as Secretary of State.

Even then, twenty years ago, it was the "sudden appearance of Germany as the grizzly terror" which "frightened England into America's arms." "For the first time in his life," says Mr. Adams, "he felt a sense of possible purpose working itself out in history." This was also the time of the Spanish War.

Next came the summer of 1900, with its fantastic doings at Peking, followed by the astoundingly successful moves of Hay — and purpose continued to shine through history. Incidentally the work was killing Hay; but was worth it.

So the diplomatic tale progresses. America learns, and so does Henry Adams, although geology and evolution still fail to solve the riddle of the World. Indeed, the Virgin, with St. Thomas Aquinas, offers more genial com-

A LAYMAN'S VIEW OF HISTORY

fort. Adams in two of his last chapters reaches some solution in "a dynamic theory of history," with "a law of acceleration" as its pivot. "To evolutionists may be left the processes of evolution; to historians the single interest is the law of reaction between force and force, — between mind and nature, — the law of progress." The United States offers, to-day, a portentous example of this acceleration of the self-consciousness of national power and world-function.

Henry Adams lived to see this, but made no attempt to include it in his *Education*. That ends with the death of Hay. Life, in thought, had never been easy to him. He enjoyed taking it very hard and then lapsing into an intellectual *laissez faire*. The latter became usual with him in the closing years. He died in his sleep. The time was that of the shattering opening of the German offensive at the end of March last. There was then warrant for what he said to his companion the day before his death: "Life has become almost intolerable."

Henry Adams is an example, so extraordinary as to be almost unique, of a New Englander who had perhaps over-considered the matter of his thought; a sophisticated mind, yet scarcely as disillusioned as it sought to think itself; nevertheless, a mind conscientiously posing as the spirit of a New England Montaigne. He avoided recognition willfully, not merely from the thoughtless, but from the sincerely thoughtful; and purposely he carried obliteration to a grave which has no stone to mark his name. None the less, the lack of recognition of Henry Adams throws a sort of faint sidelight on the culture of his country.

MONT-SAINT-MICHEL AND CHARTRES

The topic of this book is the genius of the twelfth and thirteenth centuries. Some works upon the past are history primarily, while others, primarily, are literature. In the one, the writer seemingly is lost in his subject; in the other, the subject, if not merged in the writer, at least draws interest from his personality. "The style is the man" — in literature; and in literature, it is from the "man" emerging before the eyes of our mind that we draw pleasure and illumination. Naturally, that a book is "literature" in this sense, affects its presentation of its topic. Mr. Cram says in his admirably enthusiastic "editor's note" to *Mont-Saint-Michel and Chartres:*
"Greater, perhaps, even than his grasp of the singular entirety of mediaeval civilization, is Mr. Adams's power of merging himself in a long dead time . . . it is no phantasm of the past that shines dimly before us in these magical pages; it is the very time itself in

which we are merged. We forgather with the Abbot and his monks, and the crusaders and pilgrims in the Shrine of the Archangel, etc."

In my opinion, on the contrary, we "forgather" all the while with Mr. Adams, to our great delight, if not instruction. He offers himself neither as a preacher nor a teacher, but as the "Master of the Show" which is made of the spiritual scenery of the Middle Ages. The Middle Ages are transformed in Mr. Adams's mind and mood reacting upon a period, of which he has great knowledge, and into which he has profoundly thought himself. And the book is for us a rare *trouvaille*, for whether Mr. Adams is merged in the Middle Ages, or *vice versa*, we have a moving presentation in which we hear them speak in terms intelligible to — the elect.

Who among us feels and understands the Middle Ages? Searchingly and with misgivings, the writer of this review has often asked himself this question. No Roman Catholic would admit that a Protestant, or one who had been such in his youth, could do much better than deceive himself in thinking to understand them, by conjuring up his

A LAYMAN'S VIEW OF HISTORY

artistic sympathies and interest in human striving. Can a man who does not believe in the Virgin understand the Middle Ages? Did Mr. Ruskin mean to answer this query in the negative, when he said that there had not been any noble art since men ceased to believe in Her? I do not remember just where or how Mr. Ruskin said this; but one had best not remember Mr. Ruskin too specifically, for specifically he is often wrong. One should retain him as an ennobling mood or moralizing point of view, as Mr. Adams retains him, doubtless.

On the other hand, one may doubt, and with the hope of having Mr. Adams with us, whether the true believing Roman Catholic can know the Middle Ages as well as a man who stands outside, and is not part of them, but contemplates them objectively. Perhaps in the end one is tempted, somewhat foolishly, to think that they can be understood and felt only by some ideal personage fashioned for this purpose, say one who has been a Roman Catholic and gently and sadly has very honestly ceased to believe. Might he not know them subjectively in reminiscence, and objectively in the light of clearer knowledge? As one who has ascended through a bank of morning river-fog, and can look back and see it under the sun's beams soft and white below him along the trough of the river-valley?

Mr. Adams begins with an account of Mont-St.-Michel, literary and delightful like the whole book, and then takes up the *Chanson de Roland*, as belonging likewise to the eleventh century: "The 'Chanson' is in poetry what the Mount is in Architecture. Without the 'Chanson,' one cannot approach the feeling which the eleventh century built into the Archangel's church." And he makes a finely perceptive remark in saying, "One's translation is sure to be full of gross blunders, but the supreme blunder is that of translating it at all when one is trying to catch not a fact but a feeling."

From Mont-St.-Michel, he passes through Normandy and the Ile de France, and comes to Chartres. There, fixing his abode, he will present through fascinating and suggestive chapters its towers and portals, its roses and its apse, its marvels of glass and the meanings of its legendary windows, its nave, and the church's total grand significance as the Virgin's palace-court. The popular dominance of the Virgin in medieval catholicism is given sardonic emphasis. Chapters follow entitled the Three Queens, Nicolette and Marion, Les Miracles de Notre Dame. Here the superior allure and subtlety, capacity and intelligence, veritably the leading rôle of Woman in medieval life, is made to pursue the reader through some scores of delightful pages, overflowing with intellectual whim and fantasy. The reader flees reluctantly from their captivations — their captivating paradoxes. Also the illuminating tale is told of Our Lady's inconsequent pity for the inconsequent sinners, her devotees. Judging every suppliant by his needs and love of her, Mary "embarrassed the Trinity."

With the very clever presentation of Abelard, one begins to realize the intended universality — still somewhat sardonic — of the book. And then we read the closing chapter on Saint Thomas Aquinas, and are left in doubt whether we have gone the round of the twelfth and thirteenth centuries, or the round of the mind of Henry Adams, which uses its great knowledge of that period to reflect its own reactions.

Listen to the closing paragraph of the last chapter:

"Granted a Church, Saint Thomas's Church, was the most expressive that man has made, and the great Gothic cathedrals were its most complete expression.

"Perhaps the best proof of it is their apparent instability. Of all the elaborate symbolism which has been suggested for the Gothic cathedral, the most vital and most perfect may be that the slender nervure, the springing motion of the broken arch, the leap downwards of the flying buttress, — the visible effort to throw off a visible strain, — never let us forget that Faith alone supports it, and that, if Faith fails, Heaven is lost. The equilibrium is visibly delicate beyond the line of safety; danger lurks in every stone. The peril of the heavy tower, of the restless vault, of the vagrant buttress; the uncertainty of logic, the inequalities of the syllogism, the irregularities of the mental mirror, — all these haunting nightmares of the Church are expressed as strongly by the Gothic cathedral as though it had been the cry of human suffering, and as no emotion had ever been expressed before or is likely to find expression again. The delight of its aspirations is flung up to the sky. The pathos of its self-distrust and anguish of doubt is buried in the earth as its last secret. You can read out of it whatever else pleases your youth and confidence; to me, this is all."

THE PHI BETA KAPPA IDEAL [1]

You are about to found a chapter of Phi Beta Kappa; and I am going to speak to you of the idea which is the soul of that Society. For Phi Beta Kappa is an idea, a thought. It is not of the earth — nor built of bricks and stones. Laboratories and halls are not needed by it; it does not subsist on revenues; even organizations with secretaries and presidents are only external and unessential means. For it is spiritual, and dwells in the mind.

Phi Beta Kappa is a conception of life, and then a purpose to realize it. Let us try to reach a provisional understanding of it by observing the meaning of the name — Philosophy a guide of life. Philosophy here means consideration, rational consideration. It means the scrutiny of our experiences, and the testing of their values. But this scrutiny and rational consideration do not imply that reason and the intellect are all that is of worth

[1] An address at the installation of the Beta of Texas Chapter of the Phi Beta Kappa Society at the Rice Institute, March 2, 1929.

A LAYMAN'S VIEW OF HISTORY

in a human life. Rather, a broad, rational and human consideration will embrace all human interests and experience. For our intuitions, our impulses, our passionate desires, even our loves and hates, all make part of us as men and women. They have a right to be included in the full life of a human being. That rational consideration which is philosophy will properly admit them, and ponder on their worth and truth.

But a human being, many-sided as he seems through the changing action of his faculties, is or should be a unity and a whole. He should not be a whirling eddy of distracted motives and pointless acts. Rather let him be and continue as himself. And, if so, he must keep his experiences and his thought of them integrated as elements of a whole, and related to the individual that he is. And the standard which his rational consideration must apply to his experiences is their relationship to himself and their effect upon the well-being of the whole man or woman. This is a catholic criterion by which to judge the value or the truth of anything coming into our lives. Our philosophy must regard our entire natures,

THE PHI BETA KAPPA IDEAL

and in the light of the whole consider the worth of each element of experience. To this end it must needs strengthen our character, and steady our purpose and the will to achieve it.

Moreover, no man or woman can exist alone. Individual lives are bound up in the life of society. Consequently the standard of their own welfare, which tests the worth of their experiences, must relate as well to the welfare of human society.

Such seems to me the meaning of Phi Beta Kappa and the heart of our ideal. You see at once that this conception and the purpose to realize it are scarcely inborn or implanted by nature. It does not spring up in childhood, nor is unaided youth likely to find it. It may not come to us through living out our own uninstructed lives; it must be reached through education. That will bring to us ample and well-proved matter for our thought, and will instruct and discipline us, so that we may consider everything more justly, and set it all in larger balances. Education opens to us the ever unfolding vista of the beauties and values which mankind through all the ages have drawn from life.

A LAYMAN'S VIEW OF HISTORY

Such an education will not fail to present to our minds standards of life and conduct that have been tested. These will aid us to curb rash impulses and reconsider our own most cherished whims. They will bring us matter for thought, and help us to coördinate and use it. In the end, what life has taught us, and what books have taught us, should become part of ourselves and of our working faculties and personal power. This will also strengthen our character.

I am not a professor. My years have not been passed in academic circles. But I have been a learner all my life, and have always been trying to put my thoughts together. How to teach has always been to me a mystery. I am ignorant and unpracticed in the academic art. Yet I shall venture to wander with you for a little while, through our recognized provinces of education, to find illustrations of the significance which the Phi Beta Kappa ideal carries for me.

Surely, the education corresponding with our Phi Beta Kappa ideal depends not only on the subject, but on the way each subject is taught, studied, and thought upon. The

THE PHI BETA KAPPA IDEAL

bearing and relationship of each subject to kindred matters should be made to appear. Indeed, the student should be brought to realize the inherent kinship of all manner of endeavor after knowledge. He should also try to grasp the relationship of each study to his whole education and even to his scheme of life. It goes without saying that he must use his own mind actively and constructively.

One aim of education is to draw out and develop our faculties to their utmost power. Balance and a broad foundation are important, whatever may prove to be the student's ultimate calling. If one would develop one's faculties to the full, and complete one's nature, there should be at the foundation a broad appreciation of the human elements and the enlightening influences which have built up the lives of men and women.

Those elements have been brought together for us and set forth in veritable instances and examples of their action and effect. This is the office of the great works of literature and art. They are the teachers of us all. To be sure, you do not have to read books or look at pictures in order to learn something of life. You are part of it, and it surrounds and hammers its impacts and its lessons upon you from all sides. But this does not mean that it is well for you to be ignorant of those high exemplifications of it which are likely to rise above your own experience. They may disclose reaches of humanity which you have not perceived. They will show you its greatness and beauty and open its depths; they will present its sublime attainments and awful catastrophes. They will profitably perplex your mind with mankind's dilemmas. They will teach you infinitely more than one poor life can compass in its passage through the world. Seeing, through their vision, the laws of life, you will learn to look beyond what might have been your untaught impulse and to moderate those personal whims which an ignorant person is apt to regard as true fulfilments of his nature. You will view your hopes and fears, your own small fortunes, in the universal light shed by a broad knowledge of the consequences of human conduct.

It is no light thing to learn life's lessons from these great works, any more than it is easy to learn from life itself. Education is not an easy matter; and the upward path through life, while it may be a way of happiness, is also one of unremitting toil.

As examples of such great works, I might point to the epics, the dramas and lyrics, and the art of ancient Greece. Possibly they are more beautiful and perfect than any creations since their time. They present in high relief what humanity may be and attain to through itself. They lay bare the mortal agonies of men netted in the web of fate, which is the web of their own conduct.

Modern life presses on without the Greek classics. There is no time to learn their beautiful and difficult speech. And how can we bring into our throbbing present those far-off instances of humanity, and see that it is the same as ours? Let us not waste blame upon this state of fact. Fine pictures and statues may still be seen, and the symphonies of Beethoven may be heard. There are great plays and poetry and fiction in our own tongue. These may be made our companions — the great works themselves, I say, not books about them. Read Shakespeare, Milton, if you will,

A LAYMAN'S VIEW OF HISTORY

and other splendid ones. Books about them will not make them yours.

We need these great works to complete our knowledge of what we are or may be. They give us the high features of humanity, which we are not likely to become familiar with in our daily intercourse. And they teach us the principles which control or affect the lives of all men and women. The tragedy of Macbeth shows how things come to pass; how the wicked deed breeds evil in the doer, and brings ill to all within its range of consequences. As you read the play, passage by passage, you follow the inevitable consequences of the murder of the king. Although we are no murderers of King Duncan, such great literature may enable us to see our actions set in the laws of life. In our universities today a very serious study of man and human prospects is proceeding by methods of psychology, introspective, psychoanalytic, behaviouristic, or using the pregnant concept of the Gestalt. These schools are all modern, full of energy, and doing valiant battle with each other. None of them is to be depreciated. Yet some of us are thinking of purpose and the mind's intellectual endeavors, which seem our especially human activities. Laboratory psychology has so far done little to enlighten us concerning these.

From the works of imaginative literature one passes to history by an easy transition. That also deals with life. It is not a dead, but a living record, setting forth the advances and retrogressions of mankind. It is the story of human endeavor. At least the endeavor is the most surely human part. The endeavor is the man himself. What he accomplishes or fails to do may not depend upon him.

I beg you who study history to study it with active sympathies. Bring to yourselves what the people you read about were trying to do; what they cared for; what they desired. We are judged most justly by such as understand our motives. And so one will best understand the past by looking into the motives of those who seem to have led it on, or to have held it back. We bring their conduct home to ourselves, and try to view it as if it were our own.

But we also seek in history the laws or principles of events. We cannot confine ourselves to the motive and endeavor of the actors. We must consider what they accomplished, and where and why they failed. For we seek to learn how things come to pass. And we may have noted that many a road to hell is paved with good intentions. The lesson of history is that not only must you do what seems right and best to you; but that at your peril you must choose aright, in accord with what may be the best possible outcome in the prevailing order of things.

Do we not then need all the instruction that history can bring us? We may think that the course of things does not quite repeat itself. Yet we must recognize that the courses of past events carry wisdom for us. Did I say *past* events? Is any event quite past? Rather, do not events, great and small together, carry on in their results and consequences? The past is in our present, dynamic still; even as we of the present are building ceaselessly the future, while we are doing what we can to fashion our own lives.

Our interest in history follows what we care most for in the past — that which joins with what we desire for the present, and hope for in

THE PHI BETA KAPPA IDEAL

the future. Each present shapes its own view of history, and rewrites the record according to its own desires and understanding. We care more for social and industrial affairs than for dynasties and wars. We look at politics from an economic standpoint. We take and should take from history what we care for, and can use and make into our own lives.

Here I would offer a suggestion. We want what we can use and we want the best. The epochs of the past have differed one from another. Nations and periods present elements of strength and weakness. Each great people, or notable period, has much to interest us, something to teach us. But not all of it is equally worth our notice. We should study the chief accomplishment of each people or period. By so doing we shall gain most that can be taken to ourselves.

Man is and always has been a motley animal and an aspiring soul. Rottenness and ordure strew the past. Every people, every period has its weak points, its foul parts. Their lesson is chiefly negative. We can gain more by occupying ourselves with the great and strong things of the past, than with its foolish-

A LAYMAN'S VIEW OF HISTORY

ness. Strength, rather than folly, best carries on into the making of the world.

Let me illustrate from the salient points of various peoples. We may look afar to China, and draw lessons from its old Confucian system of government and social adjustment. It can tell us of the saving strength which is held in reverence for family ties and for the graded relationships of society. We learn what conserving power may lie in customs and ceremonies.

India has quite another lesson. She reveals the need of some men to sink themselves in the calm of that which is conceived as changeless and undisturbed. Opposed to this, Greece, the universal, offers all manner of enlightenment touching the brave attempts of mortals to win whatever is of worth in human life. They strive for fame; they love all forms of beauty; they seek truth, knowledge of many kinds. Farther to the west, Rome proves her steadfast bravery; presents her self-control and her evolving methods of government; and then her admirable and cosmopolitan jurisprudence, which underlies so much of our own civil law. Passing on through the Middle Ages, we observe the constructive energies of religion, scale the heights of mysticism, and learn to feel the emotion of religious love.

The Renaissance displays the glories of religious art becoming magnificently human. We sense the reborn life of cities, and discern a strong awakening of the desire to try out the world of nature directly and through experiment. Science sturdily bestirs itself, and moves on mightily, through the centuries of Vesalius and Copernicus, of Galileo and Newton. To the north, Germany has asserted its nationality in the reform of religion and through revolt from alien ecclesiastical dominance. Among the histories of modern peoples, probably that of England can most readily be taken to ourselves; and then the story of our own expanding country. These are somewhat breathless suggestions; you will extend them for yourselves.

A knowledge of history will be found broadening and enlightening for those who enter upon the study of the law, and wish to avail themselves fully of its intellectual discipline. Nothing is better than the law to

A LAYMAN'S VIEW OF HISTORY

strengthen the reasoning faculties; and the lawyer's training and respect for precedents need not keep him from a humane and benevolent view of human affairs.

The student of history, as well as the student of literature, who would advance far, will need a knowledge of languages other than his own. That goes without saying. But, in studying languages, we must still bear in mind that our Phi Beta Kappa ideal demands that all our studies shall make for the strengthening of our faculties and the broadening of our lives. A wise and penetrating study of language is admirably adapted to open for us the ways of the human mind. It reveals the mind's spiritual energies using the images of sense — the images rising from our contacts with the physical world.

Thus far we have been busy with the humanities; that is to say, the clearly human side of education, the humane study of man, his conduct and his works. Other studies have to do directly with the world of organisms and things inorganic, in which we live. These also come within the range of our education, since no way of seeking knowledge is alien to

THE PHI BETA KAPPA IDEAL

our ideal. Only we have to think how the study of natural science may be humanized in us and made to enlarge our human selves.

I am not a scientist, and have no practical suggestions for those who are students of physics, chemistry or geology, or the biological sciences. One and all, these are entrancing fields of research and experiment. Today the old conventional barriers and divisions no longer hold between them. Physics and chemistry are but different aspects of the study of the elements and foundations of our world. Geology uses them both, and aids them in return. It is itself half biological in its investigation of the succession of once living organisms. All departments of biology need chemistry, and struggle to become exact and mathematical. They would look to the methods of physics for a pattern. But physics has recently revolutionized itself, and is passing through a region of uncanny happenings, unrealizable to any except perhaps the mathematical physicist himself. The rest of us stand without, listening to the echoes, but assured that the search itself is of the highest intellectual value.

A LAYMAN'S VIEW OF HISTORY

From our standpoint of Phi Beta Kappa, I think I may venture to say that the pursuit of any branch of science is of intellectual and human value to the man who can lift his mind to the bearing and relations of his subject. There is mental discipline in scientific work. It trains us in clear seeing, and in discriminating statement. Our scientific knowledge should instruct and enter into the principles by which we live. It will thus affect our conduct and our attitude toward every social question. I need not comment on the universal utility of science for the times in which we live.

It may be that the scientific method is essentially the same for all the sciences, however much the surface aspects vary. Always there must be some idea or working hypothesis, which suggests the line of investigation to the investigator. He uses his tools of direct investigation and carefully controlled experiment, and of mathematical calculation. He will adjust and systematize the result, but must accept what for him is the fact as he obtains it. He will reason on the fact; but, while the fact stands, it must control. Per-

THE PHI BETA KAPPA IDEAL

haps the ultimate rationale of it all is not for him. He is working in the middle distances of fact.

There is still a way of seeking truth which is not quite the same as that of science. Its emphasis is different and its scope. Science professes to confine itself to what it can see and measure, test by experiment or mathematically deduce. But philosophy, to which I now refer as the final factor in our Phi Beta Kappa education — philosophy does not recognize any such limit to its search. It is the expression of man's desire to think things out to their ultimate conclusions or despairs. Its method is rational consideration. It scrutinizes the fields of knowledge, as well as the form and substance of human experience. In its effort to certify and finally rationalize experience, philosophy may direct itself to any prevailing topic of curiosity or intellectual interest. It has, in the past, applied itself to religion, and has made religions into theologies. Today it reaches to all sides of life, and above all is absorbed with the data of science. It is seeking to test the methods and results of physical, and indeed of social, science through processes of ultimate rational consideration. Herein the imperative logic of the mind obeys its own necessities, and sets its own standards of consistency and truth.

Philosophy is for those who are moved by these insistences. I present to you its intellectual motive and answering rational effort as a proper part of your own nature, and as a final stage in your education. It will help you to appraise and harmonize the other educated portions of yourself. Philosophic consideration includes the principles of conduct and of happiness. Through these it pays due regard to all the factors of human life; it establishes the character in the fitting choice of what is best; it should enable the man or woman to think and do what is right and what seems best or most expedient through life's storms as well as under happy stars. It will help you to maintain yourself an integrated whole, a self-controlled man or woman.

Such education as I have tried to outline is merely begun in college; nor is it concluded in the opening years of professional work. It is an education to continue all your life.

THE PHI BETA KAPPA IDEAL

I have not spoken of religion, because my topic has been disciplined and integrated knowledge. But religion also moves and breathes in my own conception of a full and rounded life.

PIECES WRITTEN DURING THE WAR

THE PATHOS OF AMERICA

The American people are unconscious of their pathetic situation. Yet to perceive it requires but a moderate knowledge of the laws of life. We are the only prosperous people in the world at present. We alone are not weighed down either by war, by mobilization, or by extreme anxiety. Nor is it clearly our fault that we are fattening while the rest of the world grows lean. It is, nevertheless, portentous.

During our Civil War, some men in the North rapidly grew rich; but sacrifice kept the people chastened. Now throughout the European world an enormous castigation and, it may be hoped, purification, is taking place in which we have no share. We are not exhausting our resources for a cause, or draining our blood. Instead, we are making huge profits.

How can we help it? Are we to blame? We did not bring on the war; nor do we clearly owe to any other country a duty to take part in it. France and England cannot reasonably reproach the United States on this ground. We have no army, and but a questionable navy; there really was no way in which we could attack a foe across the ocean. And the citizens of the United States are a mixture of many peoples, with different traditions. They are, however, what they are, living in a certain organized way, through a complicated social organization, of which they are somehow part, but for which they do not seem altogether responsible. They are equipped and fitted to do the things they do; but neither fitted nor equipped for lofty sacrifice, unless, perhaps, in case they should be obviously driven to it. The machinery of their life enables them to fulfill some generous and unsacrificial instincts, and give, say, a tithe of a tithe of their profits to Belgium and France.

Let the imagination bestir itself: might not the American people have thrown a propitiatory sop to the fatness of their fate, by presenting five hundred million dollars to England and France, instead of loaning it at a good interest? Such a gift was impossible. There exists no machinery for making such a gift, but very ample and efficient machinery for making such a loan. Does not the exchange of commodities depend upon the expectation of profit? There literally exists no machinery for producing and shipping exports in requisite quantities — wheat or leather or munitions — save in the hope of profit. That hope enters into the entire process; it is an essential part of the machinery — part of our institutions, of our society, of our ineradicable motives, and of our fate. Under present conditions, the world is our oyster, and we must eat it. We must grow obese, with belly distended for some thrust of retribution, which will equalize us with humanity at large. That retribution will come in lowering of character, in loosening of sinew, perhaps in giant calamity, or perhaps not. But it will come; for we have lost our share in the strength which arises through denial and sacrifice. An Isaiah might point this out more definitely!

Conceivably some great power of motive might save us; but only a power of motive as much beyond us at present as it is a necessary part of our salvation. Above the stomach this nation scarcely exists as a nation. One must pity the United States in this world-crisis for lacking a vital motive sufficient to lift them into something above a digestive and nutritive organism. Spiritually they are footless and formless. And that there is no visible means at hand for making us other than we are, is one element of the pitifulness and pitilessness of our situation and our fate.

Again, it is not clear that we have been specifically culpable. We are netted in dilemmas of the flesh. They make our fate. And should we turn from 'fate' to God in upward yearning and in prayer, what could we pray, unless a prayer like this: Grant and fulfill, O God, the prayers that we should pray, were it not for our ignorance, and the impotence of our swinish natures. Praying thus, we should add a prayer to be made able and prepared to accept — the granting.

SUB SPECIE ÆTERNITATIS

Since the beginning of the war, thoughtful people — and I have in view primarily Americans as deeply interested neutrals — have grieved by day and in the waking hours of the night over the destruction of young and ardent life and of so much that was costly and beautiful. Will this unspeakable coil of death and ruin ever remove from our minds or be forgotten? Alas for the enormous play of hate, for the misdirection of ideals, for the world fallen in ethical pitfalls! Alas for the fatal patriotism of millions upon millions of beings so tragically mistaken! Alas for the failure to see life whole — all proportion lost in a state of *ira* which is *brevis furor!*

Our own lives are made to seem so small. How quickly would we offer them to stop the ruin! One is confused. Does the war necessitate an entire reconsideration of life? Before now, men have thought much; and we are still thinking. Are there no principles, slowly

A LAYMAN'S VIEW OF HISTORY

won from universal experience through age-long reflection, that will meet the storm?

Let us not be caught by bulk. The bigness of the war does not establish its significance. All subsequent history has proved the lasting import of Marathon — a little battle — and of Salamis. Although we cannot accept as permanently valid the declarations and assurances of those whose minds are now strained by their belligerency, their children's children will recognize whatever may prove to be the true importance of this war. At present no one can foresee wherein that will lie. This war obviously dwarfs other wars in the number of fighters, and in the altogether modern prodigiousness of the economic and social, as well as military, organization, which makes possible the fighting of such numbers; also in the new marvels of physical science applied likewise to the ends of slaughter. Possibly one great result may lie in the very demonstration of this universal organization, economic, military, scientific, and in the pregnant suggestion as to how the same hereafter may be turned to some human good. Moreover, for the time, the war has increased the

SUB SPECIE ÆTERNITATIS

world's energy by drawing out an unrealized total of devotion and self-sacrifice, which thus may be proved and made ready for employment in some clearer enlargement and ennoblement of life.

Therein lies the test. Is this war (seemingly a huge stupidity) adding to the fundamentals of life, as eminent individuals have done: scientific inventors who have facilitated physical comfort and convenience, or the far greater men who have increased the spiritual wealth of mankind? Is this world-war to have as deep an effect as Buddha, as Plato, as Jesus? One does not measure the significance of men by tons or acres, nor that of events by the noise of the concussion. The fine thought may have more lasting import than the death of ten thousand men in battle.

As for ourselves, thoughtful people who do not cease to grieve while doing what we may to relieve some infinitesimal part of the sufferings of those to whom our hearts are knit, perhaps we are entitled to some private peace of mind, which is not to be gained by turning our thoughts from the stupendous calamity.

A LAYMAN'S VIEW OF HISTORY

We are swung between unappeasable grief and the vague hopes which we are forced to visualize, so as not to despair. Consolation lies in the apparent fact that our grief has to do largely with temporal conditions, while our hopes seek to establish themselves in eternal validities. For any stable calm, the great calamity must be viewed unflinchingly. One must also look around, above, and beneath it. We must frame the conflict in larger universals, which shall span its struggling contraries and even render audible the transcendent harmony issuing from these warring opposites.

One needs faith for this final intellectual peace of contemplation; faith in the laws of life working through the tumult; faith not to worry lest the outcome shall not be just. Let no one think that he could arrange the outcome more wisely than it will adjust itself. If life is not always obviously just in its awards, it is wise beyond the imaginings of men. For it regards and makes account of the infinite web of forces which escape us; it utilizes them all, and through this measureless interrelated means, moves on along its all-considering progress.

SUB SPECIE ÆTERNITATIS

Justice is but a part. Long ago Plato taught those who would learn, that the unjust man does not benefit by his injustice, but will be injured by it as by disease; will be made worse, he himself. Here still is truth. But if the mind will span the present crisis, broader, more universal thoughts are called for, in which justice shall join with its apparently evil opposite, and the two move on in some high harmony.

Consider God, or the Sum of Power making for the coherence of the Universe, and incidentally for the checkered progress marking the record of the world we live in. The life-giving, renewing, plastic Power, or the omnipotent God, if God it be, is the God or Power of that which apparently is baneful, as well as of that which is more apparently benign: God or Power of the earthquake and the typhus-germ, and of all red-fanged nature. He or It is God or Power of the grasping, destroying, bloody ways of men, as well as of their beneficent purposes. History, both in the large and in the small, as well as we can read it, shows might triumphant, outwardly if not inwardly; lustful, grasping, destructive, *arriv-*

ing might — the might which arrives. Again and again the industry and freedom of small innocent groups have been crushed by superior force. Power in action is apt to destroy. Much of mankind's apparent progress has come independently of moral purpose, has arisen from selfish strife, and even from the triumph of the unjust cause, as it would seem.

The merely moral is not the only good! Righteousness is not the only virtue! Love is not all, justice is not all, charity, patience, humility, these are not all. It may be that in some future consummation — in the Kingdom of Heaven if one will — there is place for the fruits of wickedness, sobeit that they were begotten of power. Indeed, he who has lived out his three-score years has discovered in his own progressing selfhood, that life's whole does not lie in gladness or in sorrow only, or in duty only, or in reaching or renouncing the heart's desire, or in accomplishing the beheld achievement of the mind; but perhaps in all of these, and in much besides that seemed unrelated to any good, but rather connected with palpable lapses.

SUB SPECIE ÆTERNITATIS

Out of apparent evil, as well as out of good, life constantly advances. The horror of this world-war need not affect our faith in the purposes of God working good out of apparent evil; or, if one will, our faith in the triumphant vitality of nature and of man. There is no reason why we should not still hold fast to God, or to the eternal life-giving and restoring Power, being assured that not merely physical renewal, but some spiritual regeneration shall emerge from this cataclysm. Specifically we may still believe that the elements of culture which are not dead, but living, will renew themselves. Enough has occurred already to raise such hope to a conviction, that the suffering, fighting lands shall be benefited and renewed, each according to its need. Perhaps in them, war will purge patriotism of its grosser parts. The danger is rather for prosperous neutral countries, lest they gain nothing where they have made no sacrifice. Yet the war may purge some of their citizens of small selfishness, and help a few to the knowledge which is understanding, which is sympathy, which is love: *chi più cognosce più ama.*

A LAYMAN'S VIEW OF HISTORY

Besides the calm which comes through thought, peace may drop on the heart unexpectedly, as if straight from God's mercy. Many months ago, the fall of Antwerp was to me as the death of Bathsheba's child. I rose and returned to peace and work, after that great grief. The Greeks recognized a like peace flowing from the tragic catharsis.

Thus in two ways, which often seem to join, the way of thought and the sudden lift of feeling, one gains peace. "For we know that to them who love God, all things work together for good." Well for those who may know and feel this! For them, hate cannot triumph, nor the power of love be thwarted. But all of us can pass out beyond anxiety, through consideration of the everlasting stars and the eternal ways of the Universe which holds us all. The tragedy of our own generation may be seen set in the cycle of universal law, cause and effect, unending, infinite. What shall shatter the refuge of such consideration?

And as for concrete intruding disquietudes and sorrows,—I do not refer to closer personal anguish,—why not cry as Joinville to his knights beset by Moslem: "Let us whoop after this *canaille*, and sometime we shall be glad, telling of it in our ladies' chambers"? Or say with Æneas speaking in the storm to his companions, "Forsan et haec olim meminisse juvabit"?

THE WISDOM OF THE AGES

Since the soldiers in the trenches, as well as the rulers and non-combatants at home, desire peace, the thought arises that a force superior to their wills drives on the slaughter. The discussion of motives and purposes, of initial blood-guiltiness, serves but thinly to veil the presence of fate. We were less than men if we did not seek a reason for this apparent destiny.

The mind has been re-opened to instruction by the war — if only there were a teacher! In their spiritual helplessness, men are disposed to listen, perhaps even to the ancient voices. For the wisdom of the ages whispers still living messages, though the language may not be quite our own. Long ago, in many lands with different peoples, the consideration of life crystallized to principles and utterances, sacramental symbols of experience. Their import is one, although the phrases vary. It is the one primary lesson of cause and effect; single and universally valid in principle, though the causal nexus be ascribed to divers agencies, divine or human or material.

The symbol of life's wisdom in India was the word Karma, meaning the power of the act; the power of the act entailing its consequences from birth to re-birth, until release is won in Brahma or Nirvana. In Semitic Israel, consequences were entailed as effectively as in India; but they proceeded from the hand of Jehovah, visiting the sins of the fathers upon the children unto the third and fourth, nay, unto the hundredth generation, as we have learned. In Greece, the power of the cursed act working itself out in pain and blood, was supported by the will of Zeus. It became as infection for the unborn wicked, re-begetting itself in crime on crime. That is Aeschylean. We Christians, with our Hellenic, Jewish heritage, took from Eden a sufficiency of the same principles in the doctrine of original and ever-to-be-transmitted sin.

The snake, the crocodile, protects her young. The wolf fights in a pack; so does the German, in some respects the last word in human evolution. Through untold centuries, brute traits, brute needs have slowly humanized,

A LAYMAN'S VIEW OF HISTORY

have created institutions of the family, the tribe, the more fully developed state. There was dependence within the family; some mutual aid, some common obedience. Similar relations appear diluted in the tribe. They amplify in the monarchy or the wider empire, which must still maintain order among citizens, and may seek to promote their welfare. Yet as between different classes in the modern state, for example, civic relationships of common advantage and reciprocal exploitation often fail to rise above strained toleration, bare abstention from bloody conflict. In the course of generations, some unison of temper may result. But it is the instancy of peril from without that evokes a strong, though none too permanent, union, a union of antagonism to another state or people.

Thus mutual antagonisms keep pace with the growth of states. They make the Karma of the state, and especially of its international enmities: a Karma rising from the compulsion of antecedent violent acts; or to put it Greekly, the power of the inherent curse working itself out in crime on crime. The Jew would see it as the wrath of God visited upon the continuity of human sinfulness. Its last stage is the enormous punishment of the present war.

Is it not merited? The policy of sovereign with sovereign, of state with state, has rarely been other than rapine, scarcely mitigated by the pretentious protestations of diplomacy. No need to refer to antiquity or the Middle Ages. Look merely at the modern time, beginning, say, in the sixteenth century. Then Henry the Eighth was King of England, Francis the First was King of France, Charles the Fifth King of Spain and Emperor of Germany. Whatever good or bad these three did within their states, as towards each other they used guile and force. Italy with its popes and princes might be the spoil, and yet was no whit better than the spoiler. Since then, the dealings of king with king and state with state have risen slowly and none too surely above the standards of the hardened criminals within their borders. Their vaunted aims and policies towards each other have been such as decent individuals would blush to confess to among themselves. Superficially we ascribe this low international morality to the lack of "sanc-

A LAYMAN'S VIEW OF HISTORY

tions" in international law, which has no power to punish infringement. There is also some slackness of beneficence as between the peoples of different nations!

In our time we had thought these things were better; but the inter-state Karma was still unappeased; Jehovah had not yet sufficiently visited the sins of fathers upon the hundredth generation. Germany, impelled by antedecent guilt and a policy of blood and iron, began the war with an abominable and acknowledged crime against Belgium. If France, England, and Russia were immediately guiltless, as we think they were, they had unexpiated crimes to their accounts. Germany and Austria were the immediate criminals; but all the other nations had helped to make them such. Think of the Thirty Years' War, or the reign of Louis the Fourteenth; or of the deeds by which England made her empire. The circumstance that England for some generations has striven to rule beneficently seems not quite to have purged her Karma, judging by this war which has come upon her. There were also the Napoleonic wars at the beginning of the nineteenth century; and fifty

THE WISDOM OF THE AGES

years ago Napoleon the Little was no saint, though Bismarck proved himself the cleverer rascal.

Moreover, the state is no separate entity, but the organized aggregate of its people acting beyond their wisdom, which does not keep pace either with the increase of population or the growth of wealth and power. Shortcomings of individual human nature, or average racial nature, seem to unite with previous courses of conduct, making, as it were, a private Karma, obviously a factor in the present international result. It would savor too much of the reproaches cast by the pot upon the kettle for us to expatiate upon the imperfections of Englishmen, Frenchmen, Russians, or Italians, or of those law-abiding Germans who privately believe that the world is to be had for the taking.

So it is, to put it plainly, that man is such, and antecedent courses of human action have been such, as to result in the political conditions which the Allies, as well as Germany and Austria, must face and expiate. The ancient wisdom with its convictions of concatenation and consequence, would not pronounce those

A LAYMAN'S VIEW OF HISTORY

nations guiltless who are fighting guilty Germany and guilty Austria. And woe unto our smug selves in these United States, if we think ourselves superior. The vision is terrible: political and military history a succession of somehow tempted or necessitated acts, bringing men to a pass from which the exit leads through an unexampled horror of destruction!

Is there no help? Is no betterment somehow working itself out? No counter-Karma building itself up? Surely what has so far been said is but half. The ancient wisdom declares as well the other part, which shall be, as we hope, the sequel. For the ancient wisdom was not all held in warnings. It included hypotheses of hope. These it likewise set or symbolized in utterances which have become part of the constitution of our minds.

"From suffering, wisdom," said the Greek. "Character is a man's fate": here is promise, if the character be good. "The fate of righteous houses is blessed with fair children," still said the Greek. And the Sophoclean drama asserted a final peace of guiltless suffering, victorious over the curse of ancestral crime. Beyond these dramatic utterances, the blessedness of reason is incarnate in the life and death of Socrates.

Spiritual assurance lives and moves in Greek philosophy. The attention of the earliest thinkers was fixed upon the apparent constituency of the physical world. Their successors recognized the need of principles beyond earth's tangible elements to account for its order, if not its being. One among them launched the mind on its career as Demiurge, and prepared for the conception of divine will as Creator of the universe. Another pointed to knowledge as the steersman of human life: knowledge, virtue, happiness were at one. "From understanding come good counsel, unerring speech, and right conduct." Happiness and misery are of the soul, rather than the body; goodness lies in willing no wrong, as well as in doing none. In the following generation, Plato demonstrated the reality of mind and the creative power of its concepts. His final thought is God, pattern and fashioner of the world and man. Knowledge and virtue are the same. Justice is an excellence of man's understanding self; the unjust man is sick and miserable. The world is ruled by mind; and the human soul is indestructible.

There was always a true and a false, a better and a worse. For the great philosophers this antithesis held all life in play. They discerned it in being and non-being, in mind and matter, soul and body, knowledge and ignorance, virtue and wickedness. In holding to the nobler side of the great conflict, their philosophies fostered all the energies and faculties of man, ordering and proportioning them according to their worth. Stoicism tended to narrow the antithesis, and with it human life, to conduct good or bad. There comes an eastern or Semitic infusion, and life, reduced still further, seethes along the grooves of righteousness and sin.

The Semite's wisdom, or say the Jew's, had its own mighty assurance of victory in righteousness and love of God. He who visited the sins of fathers upon children promised "mercy unto thousands of them that love me and keep my commandments." The Hebrew religion was a religion of promise.

THE WISDOM OF THE AGES

In Jesus that promise was uplifted, and sanctified to the eternal assurance of the soul. God is spirit; his true worshippers worship him in spirit and in truth. Thou shalt love him with all thy mind and strength; ye shall love one another even as I have loved you. Christ's blessings promised the full beatitude of man's immortal part: Blessed are the poor in spirit, for theirs is the kingdom of heaven; and the merciful, for they shall obtain mercy; and the pure in heart, for they shall see God. On Jesus's message was grafted Paul's certitude that to them who love God all things work together for good; which could not be otherwise, seeing that by loving the great Purposer, man clings to the purpose and assured progress of the world.

Thus in varied language the ancient wisdom proclaims the validity and final triumph of being over non-being, of the spirit over matter and its lusts, of knowledge over ignorance, of righteousness over sin. In the glancing light of this conviction, human aspiration presses on towards the true, the beautiful, and good. It has always spurned such brute notions as "necessity knows no law," or "the end justifies the means"; whereby lusting fools over-persuade themselves of the value of the coveted end, and choose to ignore the vileness of the means. Agamemnon murdered his daughter Iphigenia in order that the winds might favor the sailing of the Grecian fleet from Aulis, — sacrificing innocent blood to bring back guilty Helen. So Germany murdered Belgium.

It is for us in the light of our extended knowledge, and with our minds incited by the war, to apply again to life the same conviction and aspiration. We must look far back in order to perceive the leading. The supporting evidence is older than the ancient philosophers and prophets had imagined. "Man was something like a fish in the beginning," said the Greek Anaximenes. We think we know this more elaborately now. The record of the earth has disclosed forms of life evolving through myriad ages, the earlier form more inchoate and elemental, with dumber faculties. Minute or vast, it was an egg-like or a bestial thing. Aeons upon aeons passed, and there came facile forms with quicker faculties, and at last the adumbration of the race of men.

THE WISDOM OF THE AGES

How long ago was that? A half a million years? It is well to speak vaguely. In that ancient aftertime we think we see the semblance of man advancing to the full human structure, crowned by a proper dome of brow, dark within as yet, and sour with savage moods. What an age-long progress and attainment, what triumph of the creative and progressive principle, of reason if one will, lay behind or within that human form divine — still none too divinely busied!

"History" reaches back a matter of six thousand years. It finds man with a soul still barbarous, in spite of gain in faculty and invention. Thinking in centuries no longer, but in aeons as we must, we realize the shortness of this historic period. Although the human advance through this small time seems marvellously quickened, these scant six thousand years are but as sunlit ripples on the floods of untold ages. A little time, in sooth, for reason to reach dominance over the age-long heritage of other instincts. Obviously, the reign of the spirit is not yet. We may even infer that God is only slowly omnipotent. His power seems not fully to control the lusts of matter and the violence of men; any more than human reason quite controls rage and bodily desire — another relatively ancient observation. Or if we would be materialists, we can think of the funny fire atoms of Democritus, which represented soul in his atomic whirl; and say these ultra-mobile, ordering, fire atoms have not, with all their extreme agility, brought to full conformity the infinitude of heavier clodlets, making the human body and the bulky world.

It is difficult to put these matters in acceptable language. We mean plainly that the progress of the world of man and God points to a time when the finer spirit of God and man shall have triumphed over the blinding desires and abominable thoughts that have produced their natural results in the present war. That peak is high and far. Impatient peace societies will vainly seek a short-cut to Pisgah. Yet the war itself may accelerate the wished-for consummation. It has shown us the astounding, yet still inchoate, progress in physical science, and has even been a factor in that advance. It has added to man's knowledge of himself, offering itself as another instance of the profound futility of violence. It has deepened our knowledge of the consequences of iniquitous action, in a way that will not be lost; and through it the world may be the wiser, as well as more expert in aviation and submarining.

And what a tragic catharsis it may prove, a universal purge of evil passion! Out of this vast, methodical violence, there has resulted an increase in the world's unselfishness, in its power of self-sacrifice. Individuals and peoples have been lifted above their ordinary self-seeking selves. This spiritual *élan* may contribute to the counter-Karma of the mind, in its conflict with the brute, and so help the moral growth of man. There is some faintest hope that the ennoblement resulting from sacrifice may prove itself in those who shall be called on to conclude a peace, and impart to these representatives of states something of the magnanimity obtaining with noble individuals. In such case, one may hope that the coming peace will be an equitable adjustment of rights and wrongs, and not an enforced acceptance of terms pregnant with retribution and revenge. A benign peace, indeed, is

A LAYMAN'S VIEW OF HISTORY

foreshadowed in the last two momentous events — results rather — of this war; the Russian Revolution and the entry of the United States.

Through the former, a cruel bureaucracy misruling in the name of a tsar, has been eliminated from the burdens of the world. The aspirations of a bounden people are loosed; and Russia is striving to establish its freedom, whatever that may prove to be. The first expressions of this new liberty have been generous. Siberian exiles are restored; the Jews have received civic rights; a suitable autonomy was proposed for Pole and Finn; arbitrary conquests are disclaimed. We watch with towering, if uncertain, hopes, and greet Russia as a brother emerging from the night, moving in a troubled dawn. We know that Karma the Inexorable is not to be dissipated, sent flying into space, by any sudden burst of good intention and reform. Only slow pain and long endeavor can eradicate the taint of tsardom and bureaucracy and the sodden inheritances of those mighty lands of present hope.

Our United States has declared war upon

the Imperial Government of Germany. Thus we vindicate our membership in the sisterhood of civilized nations, which at present is a sisterhood of furies. This kinship and participation is laden with bane and sacrifice. The righteousness of our cause does not free us from the power and presage of what we have been and still are. We have been grasping men, and our country's statecraft has not always been guiltless of the conduct that courts retribution. Now we are to make sacrifices, and perhaps suffer calamities. Let us advance with gladness towards whatever expiation is in store for us. Our entry, at least, is not prompted by greed or revenge; we believe that our minds are set upon the furtherance of the rights of peace and the delivery of the world from violence. Assuredly, we are not going to war in order to protect our commerce, or the lives of our citizens upon the seas, from the attack of German submarines. The sinking of the *Lusitania*, the more recent submarine outrages, and the espionage practised in our land, are but incidents in our resolve. We are going to war with the Imperial Government because

A LAYMAN'S VIEW OF HISTORY

of the original wickedness of its cause, the abomination of its sack of Belgium, and the continuing wickedness of its acts and purposes. Not what it has done to us, but what it is doing to the world, draws us into war. The Imperial Government knows no law beyond its will and its alleged necessities. No nation is safe from its arrogant brigandage. We fight to help the cause of right throughout the world; to protect our own democracy and insure our future safety. We hope to aid the Russian people to make strong and even holy their new-won liberty; we likewise hope to assist the German people to obtain a government which shall establish their rights and fortunes in a decent respect for the rights of others. God grant that the mind in which we have entered the war may continue pure, and that our hands may be clean at the close of our great adventure.

But admonitions from the past, and echoes of old fears within ourselves, still counsel us to preserve humility and some dread of Nemesis. Drawn within the duress and compulsion of the war, we are made bone of its bone, flesh of its flesh. Our hopes and fears for other

THE WISDOM OF THE AGES

peoples apply to ourselves along with them. For good and ill, the war has re-energized individuals and nations. Is this intensifying of power to prove an uplifting, or will the result be an equal strengthening of the animal qualities in man? Reactions come. Human nature, with all its capacity for thrills, is so elastically brutal; a weight of habit lies on us; institutions and situations, slowly evolved, have to be slowly overcome. Restraint and sacrifice are needed still, in order to rationalize, or more beneficently emotionalize, the currents of human conduct. The long path lies ahead. Our generation may tread part of it — in pain. Others will continue the march; and we, somehow, will be with them.